SEEKING SELF

an inner journey to healthy relationship

Stephan McLaughlin, Jr.

Foreword by Victor La Cerva, M.D.

HEAL

Published by
HEAL Foundation Press

Stephan McLaughlin, Jr.
Founder and Board Chair
HEAL
P .O. Box 241209
Memphis, TN 38124-1209
(901) 320-9179
www.healfoundation.org

Editor: Janette Ford Hester
Book Design: Sharaze Colley
Cover and Interior Art:
Kerry Peeples and Pam Santirojprapai
Photography: Vicki McLaughlin

Disclaimer

This book contains information gathered from many sources. It is published for general reference and not as a substitute for independent verification when circumstances warrant. The author of this book does not dispense medical advice nor prescribe the use of any technique as a replacement form of treatment for physical, mental, or medical problems by a doctor, either directly or indirectly. The author's intention is to offer tools and information to help readers in their quest for spiritual, emotional, and physical growth and well-being.

Printed in USA on acid-free recycled paper by Central Plains Book Manufacturing.

Publisher's Cataloging-in-Publication Data
McLaughlin Jr., Stephan.

      Seeking Self: an inner journey to healthy relationship/Stephan
      McLaughlin, Jr./with Foreword by Victor La Cerva, MD.
      Includes bibliographical references. First Edition.
      p. cm.
      ISBN-10: 0-9661575-2-4
      ISBN-13: 978-0-9661575-2-9
      1. Self-Awareness/Self-Introspection (Self-Help)
      2. Connection with Self (Relationship)
      3. Mindfulness/Surrender/Mind/Heart (Spirituality)
      I. Title
      2006924421

This book is gratefully dedicated to all my brothers and sisters in the Greater Human Family.

Contents

Author's Notes to Readers

The mission of our work at HEAL (Humans Everywhere Allied in Love) is to help people understand and achieve healthy relationships at all levels of human interaction. For me the essence of this work is discovering how to be more loving and nurturing to my Self and others.

Language plays a crucial role in this effort because what I say can hurt or heal. The words I use in my effort to communicate often have a dramatically different impact than I intended. I am willing to risk clarity and convention in an attempt to narrow the gap between the intention and impact of my words. Here is a brief explanation of the literary choices used in the hope of crafting a more universally respectful language for conveying the information in this book.

Use of Pronouns

The honoring of our human commonality is essential for healthy relationships. The pronouns used and references made to people were meant to be as inclusive as possible. In a few cases, quotes in the book have been adjusted to connect with a more universal audience.

With the exception of the piece of My Story found at the beginning of each of the 5 Ways, the pronouns *I* and *me* have been avoided. Because of our shared experiences on this journey, I chose to err on the side of connection, equality, and inclusiveness by using the pronouns we, us, and our. Occasional I-statements appear in the text to denote ownership of an individual meditation or practice.

Interconnectedness

Our focus on Self is not intended to promote a selfish, individualistic approach to relationship. All life is interconnected and interdependent. By focusing on one piece of the puzzle, the Self, we gain some clarity about the complexity of the human family.

Power Greater than Self

Our personal beliefs about the existence or nonexistence of a higher power strongly influence how we walk our life path. However, this is not a book about religion. My intention was to be as respectful and honoring as possible of each individual's religious beliefs, so I chose not to use specific religious terms, titles, or concepts.

Writing about the exploration of the human Self without referring to our loving nature, something I call spiritual energy, was challenging. My references to a higher power include a power greater than Self or that over which we are powerless. I invite the readers to apply their own meaning and understanding to these words.

Questions Not Answers

Explorations are about asking questions. I believe that the questions we have in common are often a stronger source of connection than the answers and that sometimes good questions are more revealing than correct answers.

Open to Other Possibilities

To avoid setting barriers, limits, or blocks and to acknowledge that there are other possibilities, the words *but, ought to, have to, must,* and *should* were not used.

The Human Handbook Series

You are reading the first book in a series of Human Handbooks, guides for creating more loving and nurturing relationships. Each future book will explore a different dimension of relationship, including those with other people, coupleship, family, coworkers, our higher power, the planet, and community. These materials are part of the educational mission of HEAL.

5 Ways to Create Healthy Relationship

The relationship with Self serves as the cornerstone for all relationships, and this book lists 5 Ways to create healthy interactions. While these Ways are not the only tools that can be used, they provide a basic starting place. Each Way offers a lesson that can be applied to the unique dynamics of the different dimensions of relationship, and their significance resonates deeper within us each time we reflect upon them and try to apply them in our life.

Foreword

by Victor La Cerva, MD

Our most basic human relationship is the one we have with ourselves. We first see our deepest nature through the mirrored reflection of those who care for and raise us. When that dance of early bonding goes well, when we have what has been termed *good-enough parents*, we are affirmed and feel in our essential being that we are worthy of love and affection. No matter our early history, each of us receives both gifts and wounds in the course of growing up. As we mature into adulthood, we gradually learn to celebrate the gifts we received and to face our dark side and do what needs doing to heal the woundedness.

Seeking Self is an offering designed to help us on this journey of inner wakefulness. It is the nature of the human condition that we are all changing and evolving. Hopefully, as a species, we pass on less confusion from generation to generation in terms of the essence of how we live our lives, seek happiness, and avoid suffering. Many beings in the world, both those experiencing abundance as well as those who do not even have the basics of what is necessary to physically survive, remain mired in confusion in terms of creating healthy relationships. We must continue to support and expand in society the development of a healthy inner life. How we hold ourselves in a loving embrace, how we experience the fine violence of breaking out of ourselves. How, most importantly, this Self-awareness, this waking up to who we really are, becomes the foundation from which we can then construct healthy families, productive communities, vibrant cultures, and a planet at peace.

Seeking Self is a primer for this important work. Forged through years of struggle, challenges, and personal growth, this book captures the profound insights we all seek on the journey. Stephan has managed to condense a lot of consciousness-nurturing tools into a clear and concise guide. The challenge for all of us is to live his words of wisdom fully, to weave into our busy and complex lives the simple answers that will bring us what we most need and yearn for: a loving and accepting relationship with our self. There is a Sanskrit term, *drala*, which roughly translates as that which occurs when the wisdom of our being is linked with the power of things as they are. It is an energy that is invoked when one is fully present, at home in one's own judgments. We need more of it in the world.

Read this book and enjoy the progress you have already made on the journey. Use the exercises and reminders to refocus on what is most important in your life. Support the important work of Heal in building healthy relationships.

Celebrate with the millions of beings who still believe in trust, compassion, joy, forgiveness, patience, and love. But, most of all, take it all into your heart and live it, moment by moment. Begin now!

Victor La Cerva, MD, has actively worked in violence prevention and is the author of several books: *Let Peace Begin With Us*, *Pathways to Peace: Forty Steps to a Less Violent America*, and *Worldwords: Global Reflections to Awaken the Spirit*. Profits from the sale of his books benefit HEAL.

Introduction

I tell you these things, not because you know them not, but because you know them. All living instructions are nothing but a corroboration of intuitive knowledge.

<small>COVENTRY PATMORE</small>

The message in this book is simple. In essence, all humans are loving beings who seek to love and be loved. However, finding love and understanding the loving nature of Self can be complicated and confusing. This handbook of Self-discovery can serve as a gentle guide for the journey.

The quest to discover our origin, purpose, and significance often begins with questions like *Who am I?* and *Why am I here?* Many share a deep desire to know more about Self or some truth yet to be uncovered. We may not know exactly what is missing, but we will know it when we see it. The answers we seek come to us in our own way and time.

This search is about overcoming the illusion of Self that has been imposed on us by others. Embedded within our essence is the innate refusal to accept the attitudes and judgments of others who wish to define us and tell us who we are, usually according to who they want us to be. Finding real Self is more about remembering who we have always been and becoming who we already are. At the end of the journey, we will know we have arrived because the reality of Self will resonate deeply and undeniably.

Like many of you, I have spent much of my lifetime seeking my Self. Many of my experiences have involved wounds and painful disappointments as I struggled to understand the dysfunctions and dis-eases in my life and relationships. Fortunately, many nurturing people appeared on my path, offering unconditional love and incredible wisdom that encouraged my learning, healing, and growth into the human being I am today. They shared information with me in an open manner, without expectations or demands, and honored my ability to apply what was offered in my own way.

My personal journey and divine guidance have inspired the creation of *Seeking Self,* a collection of 5 Ways to clarify and strengthen healthy relationship with Self. My intention for this book is that it might serve as a source of support to others on their life journey.

If I had wanted to entice people to read this book, conventional wisdom would have been to *wow* readers with my credentials and accomplishments, while glossing over my failures. Initially, I resisted telling My Story because I felt the personal details would get in the way of creating a tool that would have universal appeal and utility. However, my friends and collaborators reminded me of the effectiveness of giving examples and telling real stories. I remembered learning great lessons from individuals who had owned and shared their struggles with me. So, at the beginning of each chapter I have included pieces of My Story in which I own and share how each Way transformed my relationship with Self.

Each of us is a teacher and a student. Knowing that we teach what we need to learn, this book is my humble attempt to share with you the loving gifts and support that were so generously shared with me. I am a life-long learner and an explorer who does not presume to have all the answers. If I have learned anything about healthy relationship, it is to trust that readers will apply to their lives whatever in this work is of value to them.

My life lessons have been as much about unlearning old ways as about opening up to new wisdom and possibilities. What I once believed was valuable and important has been supplanted by new values that I know with every fiber of my being are authentically worthy and rich. I have learned what a relationship *could* be rather than what it *should* be. The information, insight, and understanding that I have gained transformed my journey from a fear-centered path leading to early destruction, darkness, and death to a love-centered way filled with more light, hope, health, and inner harmony than I ever imagined.

We are in the midst of a global shift that is establishing a common ground for a more love-centered way of living, thinking, and relating. Who we are, why we are here, and the secret of Self can be found within each of us, ready to profoundly transform our life and relationships. My intention is to inspire you to seek your authentic Self, discover your inner workings, and create more harmony and peace in your life. Thank you for joining me as we explore, discover, and realize the magnificence of what it means to be a loving human being, a Self. May you love and be loved.

SEEKING HARMONY,

The answer lies within
So why not take a look now?
CAT STEVENS

WAY 1

AWAKEN AND
EXPAND AWARENESS

And so in order to wake up, the one thing you need the most is not energy, or strength, or youthfulness, or even great intelligence. The one thing you need most of all is the readiness to learn something new. The chances that you will wake up are in direct proposition to the amount of truth you can take without running away.

ANTHONY DeMELLO

My Awakening

Like many middle-class American males, I was busy for the first 35 years of my life trying to measure up to the expectations of my family, community, and country, despite their judgments and shaming of my accomplishments. For 15 of those years, I worked tirelessly toward achieving the great American Dream. Working physically and mentally hard to achieve big business success and make money, I felt vividly alive and empowered. There was no word in my vocabulary for slow, just go, go, go.

In pursuit of that dream, I gathered a team of passionate, intelligent young people, and together we struggled to build a successful company. Every day was filled with new challenges and problems, and, as fast as they popped up, my associates and I dealt with them. Although the workdays and nights were very long, the entrepreneurial ride was exhilarating and intoxicating, and our fast track to success seemed to be worth the price.

My life was a balancing act that I managed well, or so I thought. During the week, I took care of myself by eating well and exercising; yet, I played hard and partied late on most weekends. During these years I relied on a self-destructive diet of medicating substances to mask my dysfunctional behaviors and to soothe and renew my body and brain for the never-ending rounds of 12-hour, crisis-filled workdays. Too tired to notice my increasing stress level and too obsessive-compulsive to slow down, my fear of failure kept me running just ahead of my shadows. I was blind to the darker side of what was really happening in my life and unaware of the negative costs incurred by my choices and beliefs.

Then, with little warning, life presented two startling events that wrenched my attention back into the present. First, a big company came along and offered us a cash buy-out for the business. Second, my father, who had been ill for several years, suffered an unexpected fall and died within a few weeks. Somehow, I moved through this contrasting experience of devastating loss and ultimate abundance. I supported my father as he succumbed to death, while simultaneously navigating the complexities necessary to reap the rewards of many years of hard work.

Although the business transition went smoothly, administering my father's last will and testament and his expectations of me as executor set the stage for a frightening chapter of family history. This legacy included dealing with money issues that eventually led to a struggle with one of my brothers. The more he insisted, the more I resisted, and we arrogantly tried to impose our personal perspectives on each other. Although our dangerous drama for ultimate control nearly escalated into lethal violence, I did not want to kill my own brother, even in self-defense.

Despite my intense feelings of anger and fear and my best efforts to settle the conflict without a fight, the situation only got worse. My helplessness turned into panic, and I steeled myself to fight for my life. As our standoff reached a climax, something incredible happened. Feeling totally overwhelmed, I woke up one morning and resisted the seduction of the struggle. I stopped fighting, opened my heart to new possibilities, and chose to let go of winning and being right. Instead of trying to fix the problems alone, I asked for help. Without realizing it, my awakening and surrender had begun.

By the grace of a power greater than my Self and an intervention led by a wonderful man named Pete Parker, my family and I were led to a special place of healing. We were welcomed at the entrance of the treatment center by a prophetic sign that read: *Expect a Miracle.* Despite my initial reluctance, I remained open to healing, and the darkness of egotistical illusion slowly transformed into the light of recovery and reconciliation. Later, as I was leaving the facility, I read the blessing on the reverse side of the entrance sign: *YOU are the Miracle!* These gentle, loving words became a touchstone for my inner journey.

My awareness of what was happening in my life led to big changes and new opportunities for healing. I slowed down and began to live in the present moment. The life that had been filled with fear and doubt was transformed into a life of love and trust. My awakening was like a shock because my world suddenly looked so dramatically different.

It was a good difference, though. In the old, fear-dominated days, I used my beliefs and assumptions like stones to build walls around myself. Waking up stirred a great upheaval in me that knocked down these old, protective barriers. As these stones came tumbling down, they formed a new, love-centered foundation, a road that supports rather than suppresses me and frees rather than isolates me. My expanded awareness inspired meaningful changes in my life and lay a path that I now walk as I seek my Self.

Way 1: Awaken and Expand Awareness

*Each of us knows all. We need only to open our minds
and hearts to hear our own wisdom.*

THE BUDDHA

There are many paths to healthy relationship with
Self. This one begins when we are willing to
take a deep, courageous look within our own interior. In
today's busy, demanding lifestyle, many of us are eager to
presume that a quick completion of our personal *to do list*
will put us on the fast track to health and happiness.

Whether we seek to heal internal wounds or to grow
into our full potential, finding wholeness and fulfillment
requires that we pay more attention to the little things
that are happening inside us right now. This subtle and
valuable information is incredibly easy to miss as we
cruise past unnoticed details of life and relationship. Too
often, we are not willing to slow down and take a peek
inside. Only when reality bites through some tragedy,
emergency, or dilemma do we face ourselves with full
attention.

Fortunately, there may be an easier way to awaken
our consciousness and expand our awareness. The choice
to read this book is a conscious intention to accept the
challenging adventure to discover the meaning of being
human. When we slow down, open up, and pay attention

to the little things, something new and wonderful happens in our lives. Thus begins the inner journey, the seeking of Self.

Learning to calm our inner turmoil makes it possible to observe and appreciate more of what is happening within and around us right in this very moment. New clarity comes with this heightened sensitivity, revealing the hidden meaning of our words, actions, and feelings. Relationship with Self is shaped by the choices we make in the present moment. As the consequences of these choices become apparent, we are empowered with the wisdom to more consciously and intentionally create the quality of relationship we desire and deserve.

Our inward journey embraces the value of each moment. Awakening and expanding awareness deepens our sense of Self, spiritual connections, and personal experiences. **If we are willing to open our eyes, ears, mind, and heart to the little "overlooked" things, we can realize our potential to become more nurturing beings and compassionate partners in all of our relationships.**

Slow Down

We are not able to slow down the hectic pace of the world,
but we can slow ourselves down and notice and reflect
upon our experiences. Then they will have value
and meaning for us.

TOUCHSTONES

Are we busy because we have to be or because we want to be? Is there a payoff for living a hectic, rushed life? Our motivation for completing important tasks can vary from honoring valid commitments to avoiding other activities, especially our own internal issues. **Busyness is a choice. Altering behavior patterns can change the pace of our lives and may be as simple as making the choice to slow down.**

We complain about being too rushed and having too much to do. Yet, how often do we just say no? Is there a *prize* or a *price* for winning the human race? Maybe we are fortunate just to be participants. When we make choices that slow down our lives, the little things in the present moment that give meaning to our interactions are easier to notice and appreciate.

In physics, the Theory of Entropy states that there is a universal tendency of matter to seek a less ordered state. In a similar manner, our lives seem to become increasingly chaotic the busier we get. This is particularly true as we

AWAKEN
AND EXPAND
AWARENESS

make the transition from childhood to adulthood and begin to accept responsibilities, commitments, and consequences. Although we may have no power over how quickly world events develop, our expanded awareness gives us the power to join the fast-paced excitement of modern life or to make choices that reduce the external forces that push and pull us into its hectic flow. Healthier choices can slow down our lives, thereby preserving our integrity, sanity, and internal calm.

Time is precious and flows relentlessly. Many of us are overcome by the urgency not to waste it. However, finding the balance between a less hectic life and moving quickly when appropriate can be challenging.

Read the lists on the following pages of familiar behavior patterns we often choose. One list of choices can make life stressful, while the other offers more time for appreciating life experiences. Slowing down could alter our lifestyle, creating more time and space to form authentic, richer, and healthier relationships.

Choices That Speed Up My Life

My life tends to speed up when I…

…try to accomplish too many tasks.

…attempt to control things over which I have no power.

…attempt to control or "fix" other people and their problems.

…try to prove my worth to people who do not share my values and passions.

…struggle to reach the unhealthy expectations set by my family, friends, community, and Self.

…work to earn money to acquire material items that I do not really need or use often.

…agree to activities in order to please or avoid upsetting others.

…make commitments without fully understanding the effort, costs, and consequences.

Choices That Slow Down My Life

My life tends to slow down when I…

…attempt to accomplish fewer tasks while being more present in the moment.

…surrender control over that which I have no power, especially other people.

…make healthy choices for my life and relationships.

…connect with people about whom I really care.

…appreciate the relationships, health, and happiness that I already have.

…joyfully fulfill my healthy responsibilities as I understand and accept them to my family, friends, workplace, and community.

…choose work that is enjoyable and fulfilling.

…buy material items that I really need and use.

…set boundaries to protect my integrity and create realistic, healthy commitments.

…disengage from relationships that are not loving and nurturing.

…risk upsetting others by first taking care of my Self.

Breathe and Relax

Breath is life. Breathing is nature's way of renewal. We release stale energy and feed ourselves with life force. Shallow or tight breathing makes us sick; full and easy breath keeps us healthy. Usually we are not aware of our breathing. But when we turn our attention to it, something magical happens. Our breath becomes slower, deeper, and we sink into a different state of consciousness.

LOUISE DIAMOND

Busyness, expectations, and over-reaching are just some of the choices we make that cause stress and tension in our life. Such choices block our breath and, consequently, the flow of our mental, emotional, and spiritual energy. Breathing, meditating, and reflecting are techniques that calm and relax us, relieve tension, remove blocks, and encourage the flow of oxygen. Choosing to breathe and relax can open us up, clear our body and mind, and greatly enhance our awareness.

Relaxing can be as simple as taking a little time to be quiet and still. For some of us, this is difficult. Our thinking mind resists unwinding and slowing down, unless we are asleep or our attention is suppressed by some diversionary activity, like watching television. Napping, daydreaming, breathwork, meditation, yoga, and visualization are ways to relax without numbing or dulling our senses. During meditation, for instance, we can choose to release attachment to the many thoughts that vie for our attention. This practice sends the message to Self that we have done enough for the moment and deserve a break.

Relaxing includes other physical and mental activities that stimulate our body and free our mind. Walking, reading, watching films, listening to music, playing an instrument, drawing, painting, dancing, martial arts, games, and sports are relaxing ways to play and have fun. Taking time everyday to relieve stress benefits our personal well-being.

Breathing is exhaling and inhaling. The outflow of old, stale air makes room for the inflow of new, fresh air and releases the accumulated stress of daily living. **Breathing renews life and strengthens vital internal connections between the physical, mental, emotional, and spiritual parts of Self.** The practice of watching the movement of our breath is called breathwork. In this calming silence, our inner workings are easier to perceive.

Meditation is a practice that builds on breathwork. **As we turn our attention inward on our breathing, we may notice how our busy mind keeps us in an invisible state of tension and anxiety.** By allowing our thoughts to come and go and not getting attached to specific outcomes, we realize we are not what we think. Letting go of our thoughts can be freeing and calming. A less formal way of watching our breath and thoughts is called reflection. Like meditation, reflection soothes us as we quietly sort through the clutter of our mind.

Following are some examples of ways to practice breathwork, meditation, and reflection. At first, our attempts to slow down may seem to backfire as we experience more, rather than less, mental activity. This is a natural consequence of paying more attention to all that is happening just below the surface. If we are gentle and patient, the benefits of breathwork can be ours.

Breathwork for Beginners

Find a quiet place.
Sit comfortably.
Close your eyes.
Begin to breathe.
Place both hands on your belly.
Gently push in.
Exhale.
Take in a full, deep breath.
Inhale.
Make a long, sighing sound.
Exhale.
Breathing only through your nose,
take several slow, shallow breaths.
Breathe steadily and rhythmically.
Notice your breath as it enters and exits your nostrils.
Count your breaths slowly - 1, 2, 3, 4.
Repeat.
Relax your body and release tension.

Meditation for Slowing Down Busy Minds

Start with breathwork.
Watch your thoughts as they go by.
Without trying to stop them, just watch.
Let them stream, connected to each other.
Notice the space where one thought ends and another begins.
Increase the length of this space.
Spend more time in this space between the thoughts.
See how long you can make these spaces last.
Practice accepting where you are in this moment.

Meditation for Renewal

Start with breathwork.
Breathe out old, warm, stale air.
Breathe in fresh, cool, life-giving air.
As you exhale, visualize breathing out negative energy.
As you inhale, imagine breathing in positive energy and hope.
Exhale darkness.
Inhale light.
Exhale fear.
Inhale love.

Try the following exercises. Add or substitute words that represent your own releasing and renewing qualities in a personal setting. Take one quality at a time and breathe out the negative and then breathe in the positive.

Meditation For Work

Breathe out chaos.
Breathe in order.
Breathe out confusion.
Breathe in clarity.
Breathe out frustration.
Breathe in patience.
Exhale stagnation.
Inhale freedom.
Exhale boredom.
Inhale fascination.
Exhale conflict.
Inhale collaboration.

Meditation For Home

Breathe out the desire to criticize and judge.
Breathe in acceptance and unconditional love.
Exhale stress.
Inhale tenderness.
Exhale tension.
Inhale calm.
Exhale anger.
Inhale joy.

These exercises can be used to help us relax, to remain centered when anger buttons are inadvertently pushed, or to fall asleep after being awakened by fear or anxiety in the middle of the night.

Choosing to relax in ways that work for us can literally provide a little breathing room in our lives for a fresh perspective. Breathing, mediating, and reflecting relax us so we can see more clearly through the fog of our own busyness, fears, and doubts. We become more centered, alive, and aware when we give ourselves the gift of our own attention.

Awaken
and Expand
Awareness

Become a Keen Observer

If I were to begin life again, I should want it as it was.
I would only open my eyes a little more.
JULES RENARD

As we awaken, the haze of life's stress and busyness begins to dissipate, and we are able to see our relationships more clearly. Each of us can become a great detective like Sherlock Holmes or Hercule Poirot, collecting information methodically, passionately, and with the purpose of solving a great mystery. Like these keen observers, we look for the subtle clues in our moment-to-moment interactions, hoping they will reveal essential information that we may have been missing. **We can learn to allow life to unfold and resist the temptation to make false assumptions or to respond impulsively without first evaluating all the evidence.**

As relationship detectives, we rely on awareness and keen observation to thoroughly glean the details from each encounter. **Facial expressions, tears, volume and tone of voice, body language, fidgety fingers, and eye contact reveal possible internal turbulence. Compassionate consideration of these telltale signs could unveil the mysteries that motivate us to behave as we do.**

To hone our observation skills, try the following exercises. Breathe, relax, and give attention to all the new, little details of each experience. Do this alone or with a trusted friend. With full attention, notice the previously unnoticed. Silently answer each question, one at a time. Return the favor and test the skill of your friend. Sharing this exercise with someone enhances the experience and brings up details that may have been missed.

There are so many little details that it is difficult to notice them all. However, when we take the time to look for them, these new features enrich each experience. On our inner journey, we realize there is much more about observing Self than meets the eye.

Observe Your OUTER Self

Look into a mirror.
What do you see?
What was your first thought?
Was it a judgment, criticism, or compliment?
Check out your hair.
Name the color of your eyebrows.
Observe the shape of your nose.
Notice the wrinkles and lines of your face.
Look at your eyes.
Are they happy or sad?
Look at your mouth.
Is it smiling or frowning?

Observe Your INNER Self

Sit quietly with your eyes closed.
What do you see now without using your eyes?
Do you see patterns and colors on the inside of your eyelids?
What is happening in your head?
Is your thinking slow and calm or rapid and chaotic?
How deeply are you breathing?
Does your breath stop at the top of your lungs?
Can you feel the air warmly filling your lungs?
Now look even deeper within.
Can you feel your heart?
How fast is it beating?
How are you feeling at this very moment?
What do you need right now?

Practice Being More Fully Present

Relationship can be a devotional, spiritual practice of awakening. When we are really able to see with the heart… we are filled with gratitude for the truth and beauty for what is present, now in this moment.

Victor La Cerva

Being fully present focuses our whole attention on the immediate interaction in which we are involved. In this moment, right this second, we can expand our awareness of the physical, mental, emotional, and spiritual details of our relationship experiences, especially our *inner* action with Self.

People are often indignant at the suggestion that they might not be living in the present. While true that the human body has the limited ability to be in one place at a time, the mind, heart, and spirit have the flexibility to wander and roam. Not living in the present can be described as a detached, preoccupied way of existing that gives only half-hearted attention to the richness of our life experiences and the attributes of Self. Although certain events and personal interests can pique our attention and temporarily bring us into the present moment, the auto-pilot engages easily, allowing us to slip back into a state of less conscious living. This form of escapism can become so habitual that we do not even realize it is happening.

Not living in the present moment is rarely a choice we consciously make. Like the daydreamer's subtle drifting out of awareness, we evade the now. **We learn to escape the uncomfortable challenge of change, to avoid the disquieting energy of a feeling, or to resist the nagging persistence of an unsatisfied need.** Dwelling in the past, nursing our regrets, and spending time in the future worrying about events that may never come to pass are common ways to stay out of the moment. Other familiar ways we trick ourselves into being less than fully present include excessive work, exercise, housecleaning, and talking. More extreme examples include obsessive thoughts, compulsive behaviors, codependent focus on other people, and the full menu of addictions that effectively block us from experiencing our lives in real time.

These habits can be costly. We risk our health, relationships, and happiness. Without even noticing, we

become numb to our internal experiences. Such repetitive behavior patterns can create unnecessary tension in our bodies and lead to physical maladies and missed opportunities to share meaningful experiences. The first opportunity missed is the chance to connect with Self.

Making conscious, healthy choices leads us back to the present. The following activities can help us develop skills for becoming more fully present.

Breathwork	*Martial Arts*	*Sports*
Counseling	*Meditation*	*Support Groups*
Exercise	*Reflection*	*Yoga*
Journaling	*Relaxation*	

These practices bring physical, mental, emotional, and spiritual benefits into our lives as we learn to…

> *…relax and calm down.*
> *…focus on breathing.*
> *…let go of distractions.*
> *…raise our conscious awareness.*
> *…get energy unstuck and flowing.*
> *…remove internal barriers and blocks.*
> *…give our attention to details of the moment.*
> *…integrate new habits into daily life.*
> *…commune with nature.*
> *…be silent.*
> *…practice nonjudgment.*

For centuries, people all over the world have used these methods to increase their awareness of the little things, to receive the gift of their own attention, and to savor the serenity of being fully present. The dreams that may be manifesting in our lives at this very moment can be experienced and enjoyed when we are willing to live more fully in the present.

Be Open to New Possibilities

*Nothing new can happen in your life until you
clear out the space for it.*
DON JONES

As seekers of Self and adventuresome, life-long learners, we are willing to ask questions and look for new ways to live life more fully, even if we see ourselves as content and fulfilled. **When we risk opening up and becoming vulnerable, new things can happen in our life.**

Imagine a vessel full of water. If we try to pour additional water into this full glass, it spills over the sides and is lost. The fresh water can be retained only after discarding some of the old. We, too, are vessels and are often filled to capacity. Our mind, heart, and life may be filled with regrets about the past, worries for the future, and old thoughts, beliefs, assumptions, and experiences that prevent new possibilities. Changing any of our accumulated knowledge and assumptions may not be desirable. However, even small shifts can reward us with more authentic, intimate connections with Self.

Opening up may be as simple as trying on new clothes. We could consider different perspectives or try on new concepts, keeping only the ones that fit. The practice of being more fully present through relaxation, breathing, and meditation opens us up so that we can allow

AWAKEN
AND EXPAND
AWARENESS

the previously unnoticed and unappreciated. Perhaps we could notice or be grateful for the message in a feeling, the blessing of some time alone, the chance to attend to a neglected need, an opportunity to share a burden with trusted friends or just to listen to a stranger.

Releasing the old stimulates new experiences and opens us in loving and nurturing ways. A quiet, open Self is more prepared to receive and process than a closed and cluttered one. Wonderful things can happen when we give ourselves permission to open up to new possibilities.

Wonder Why

Wonders never cease, if one never ceases to wonder.
ZIGGY

The search for an understanding of Self begins with the simplest of questions. *Who am I? Why am I here? What is my purpose?* Curiosity about our existence guides our exploration of the outer world and beckons us on the inner journey. These questions weave a common connection that unites us as one Greater Human Family.

Many wonders of our humanness occur beneath the surface, just out of sight. Relying exclusively on observable activity in our relationships, like behavior, provides only a small slice of the awesome complexity and beauty of what it means to be human. Exploring Self involves looking above and below the surface in an attempt to understand who we are and how we work.

Here are a few questions that will illuminate our way. Why do we do the things we do in our relationships? How do we get the love and the quality of relationship that we want? Which actions bring us closer to our vision of the person we want to be, and which ones deter the realization of our goals and desires? Why do we have these strange happenings called feelings? What are they trying to tell us?

These insightful questions do not lend themselves to quick, one-time answers. **Rather, they are lifetime inquiries that invite us to look for a new, deeper understanding of Self. Asking them again and again is essential because the answers reveal themselves slowly over time to those who are willing to explore and work to understand and apply their secrets.** Listening to the answers without judgment or criticism of our thoughts, feelings, wants, and needs enhances our understanding of the dynamics at work. The wonders of Self never cease if we are only willing to continue to wonder.

Regard Each Day as Sacred

When I think about my days, almost any day, I think about not having enough time…a small shift made me see that if I can't do everything at once, I can do many of the things I want if I am willing to give them space and time and patience.

SUE BENDER

D o we confuse the passage of clock time with LifeTime? Clock time is made up of seconds, minutes, and hours that we use to manage the many activities of the calendar. LifeTime consists of the small pieces of moment-to-moment existence in which we have an opportunity to take notice or action. Segments of clock time line up to form a measure of our past and present. LifeTime, one of our most valuable resources, is that brief piece of existence in which our spiritual essence occupies our human body.

LifeTime is all the time we have to be with the people and things we love, and it can end in an instant. Clock time is infinite, while LifeTime is finite. Like any resource, the manner in which we use it often depends on how much we think we have. If we assume we do not have an endless supply of LifeTime, we might value and utilize it more fully.

How valuable is our LifeTime? Do we realize that each choice we make to use, give, or share it consumes a portion of this precious resource? Are we unconsciously squandering this gift by confusing activity and busyness with accomplishment? No human has the power to create more time. Yet, by slowing down and being more fully present, we honor the sacredness of LifeTime.

Our old perception of time could be altered radically if we suddenly learned that we had only a small amount of it remaining. Usually, our lives are lived without such information, not knowing when our words or actions might be our last. If we believed our time was limited, we might pay closer attention to the LifeTime left and strive to make our words and actions much more meaningful. Under these circumstances, we would acknowledge the sacredness of each day.

Major changes in our relationship with time might help us to more fully appreciate the significance of our daily allocation. There are simple ways we can honor the value of LifeTime and take greater care in how we spend it. **Learning to give our whole Self – heart, mind, body, and spirit – to every experience and encounter of each day manifests the sacredness.**

How does this awareness affect the quantity and the quality of time we spend with ourselves? Starting the day with quiet time for mediation and reflection is a simple way we can cherish the valuable gift of time with Self and others.

Although tomorrow may hold potential richness, the experiences of today could be all we were meant to receive. The miracle in every moment of LifeTime makes each day sacred.

Reflections for Daily Sacredness

Treat every waking moment
as if it were the most important moment in your life.

Acknowledge and affirm your Self
as being "good enough" and an important contributor to
your own growth and well-being.

Remind your Self that your life matters
and others love and depend on you.

Connect with your Self
by expanding awareness of your inner "action."

Treat any farewell
as if it were the last opportunity to tell others
how much you care.

Awaken
and Expand
Awareness

Check Out the View

Remember always that your mind must be like a room with many open windows. Let the breeze flow in from all the windows but refuse to be blown away by any one.
MAHATMA GANDHI

No matter how keen our awareness, there are some parts of Self we cannot see, depending on our point of view. For a surprisingly novel look, check out the views of Self through the Johari Window. Given its name in 1961 by psychologists Joseph Luft and Harry Ingram, this four-paned "window" is a revealing tool for Self-awareness and exploring interpersonal relationships.

Each of the four windowpanes consists of two enlightening perspectives of Self. The first is how we view Self by using the information we know and perceive about our Self. The second is the viewpoint of us as seen by others who use the same information that they, too, can perceive or know.

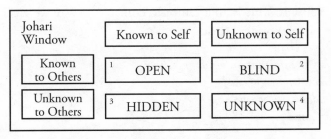

Johari Window	Known to Self	Unknown to Self
Known to Others	1 OPEN	BLIND 2
Unknown to Others	3 HIDDEN	UNKNOWN 4

OPEN: The view from this windowpane is information that we know about our Self and is also known by others.

job or work
pastimes
physical appearance
shared personal history

skills
the person we present to the
   world
the public Self

BLIND: The next windowpane represents the information that we do not see about ourselves but that other people can detect.

abilities
arrogance or conceit
fears
feelings
generosity
habits or hang-ups

humility
leadership qualities
neediness
resentment
selfishness
weaknesses or character defects

HIDDEN: This windowpane is comprised of that which we know about Self but others do not, until we choose to disclose it. This is an attempt to control the way we wish to be seen by the world.

private information we do not share
secrets held consciously
shadows, things we hide or deny
unshared personal history

UNKNOWN: This windowpane contains information about us that we do not see and neither do other people.

creativity
denials
forgotten personal history
frustrated needs
repressed memories

shadows, things we suppress
suppressed feelings
undeveloped talents, abilities,
  or interests

Many of us may have chosen consciously or unconsciously to hide, deny, suppress, or forget certain parts of our behavior or history in an attempt to avoid discomfort or pain. Unfortunately, just because we choose not to see a behavior, feeling, or need does not make it go away. The undesired effects of these choices may show up in our lives as unusual behaviors, consequences, or reactions. Whether we are suffering or just not content, we may find the causes of our problems or sensitivity hidden in some less visible parts of Self.

Connect Deeply

You will connect with a fresh vision of your child, enriched by your years of adult experience. This is your true homecoming. It is a discovery of your essence, your deepest, unique self.

JOHN BRADSHAW

According to an old Native American legend, there was once a dream-inspired, prophetic petroglyph that foretold of the coming of a strange, new people to the land. This rock drawing depicted a human figure whose head was not attached to its body but, instead, was floating above its torso. The drawing symbolized people who had lost their essential mind and body connection. This separation of the feeling-body from the thinking-head represented an ominous loss of sensitivity and spirituality that would ultimately spell disaster and the near total destruction of the Native American people.

The disconnection of heart and head was caused by a loss of awareness, the result of the so-called civilized lifestyle of the newcomers. Some of those same forces are at work in today's world. **Although more intelligent and informed than ever before, we can be lost in thought.** Separated from the energy and sensations of our human experiences, we may suffer a loss of connection to something greater than ourselves. This ancient vision serves as an apt metaphor to remind us that we are so much more than merely thinking beings.

Eckhart Tolle, a contemporary spiritual teacher who is not aligned with any particular religion or tradition, implies in his writings that spiritual awareness begins when we realize that the human experience exceeds the limits of human thought. Reuniting our head to our body connects our thinking Self with our physical Self. Deeper in the body resides the parts of us that are difficult to see and understand. Here, too, lies other, more ancient ways of sensing worldly experiences. **When our mental capabilities are deeply connected to our emotional nature, we are more aware and authentic.**

The deeper we go, the more we find. Beyond thought and emotion lies another subtle aspect of Self, our spiritual nature. Throughout human history, spirituality has been the subject of intriguing, often intense, debate. Such words as life force, spirit, soul, *ki, chi, prana, ruh,* and others have been used to describe that deeper aspect of being. These names attempt to honor something that happens when we combine head and heart, a deeper connection which is greater than the sum of the parts and unifies us into a more whole, integral Self.

Our inner journey focuses on the delicate dance between the mental, emotional, and spiritual aspects of our humanness as we seek to connect deeply with Self and understand what it means to be fully human.

Way 2

Find Personal Power

The more you connect to the Power within you, the more you can be free in all areas of your life....We must be willing to release the patterns in our lives that are creating conditions we say we do not want. We do this by going within and tapping the Inner Power that already knows what is best for us....Life is a voyage of self discovery. To me, to be enlightened is to go within and to know who and what we really are, and to know that we have the ability to change for the better by loving and taking care of ourselves.

Louise Hay

My Surrender

My earliest recollection of power was the ability of adults to override my choices with their own. With some resentment, I accepted that this was how power worked and would soon learn to assert my own personal power in much the same way.

By the time I reached my early 20s, I was carrying a huge bag full of powerful choices that I believed belonged only to me. The measure of my worthiness was directly linked to the number of choices I made as a man, a boss, and a steward, especially those concerning other people and the events in their lives. My illusion of personal power presumed that I was supposed to take care of other people, fix problems, and be strong, decisive, hard, and domineering, whenever necessary. While this belief was reinforced by my sincere desire to help other people, it fostered a potentially harmful attitude that I had all the answers. No matter how honorable my intentions, this misuse of my personal power caused problems rather than solved them.

Like many young men, I was trained to be a warrior. I barely missed being drafted into the Viet Nam War, so I created my own war. My battleground became the business world, where victory was measured in dollars and success meant being good enough, especially in the eyes of my family. Instead of order and peace, I found myself surrounded by chaos and negative conflicts, like the intense confrontation with my brother. I could not afford to break down; however, I *had* to break down. My choices to stop fighting and to accept that I was powerless over him were my first surrenders.

Fixing my brother was my initial reason for going to a treatment center with my family; it had nothing to do with me. Although I behaved and used substances addictively to relieve the pain of my battle wounds, I could not see that I, too, had a problem. My denial was based on my fear of failure and appearing weak, inept, and unworthy. My surrender continued, and I admitted my powerlessness over my life and the people in it. This was the first of my twelve steps towards recovery and a new life.

My next surrender centered on my work habits. As I got clean and clear, the connection between my choice to work too much and my lack of harmony became more obvious. Not only did I medicate by using drugs, I medicated with work. Unlike other destructive addictions, workaholism was accepted, condoned, and even encouraged by my family and community. The loss of spirituality I suffered as an addict paled in comparison to the huge chunk of life that was lost while working to achieve the so-called American Dream.

Once again, I had to let go. This time I turned over all my beliefs about work to a power greater than myself and immediately experienced a huge sense of relief. It was time for me to stop trying to take care of others and just accept the love and nurturing I needed as a simple human being. For me, serenity and peace became something granted, not achieved.

Sometimes I still associate being loved and good enough with carrying great responsibility. Today, the difference is that I seek to surrender, encouraged and supported by guides and companions who accept me right where I am without shame or judgment. Now I find my personal power through my choices of acceptance, attitude, mission, humor, love, gratitude, and service.

FIND
PERSONAL
POWER

Way 2: Find Personal Power

We have power aplenty, but we must exercise it in order to understand its breadth. We'll find all the day's activities, interactions, and plans decidedly more exciting when we exercise control over our responses. We are strengthened each time we determine the proper behavior, choose an action that feels right, and take responsibility where it is clearly ours to take. The benefits will startle us and bring us joy!
EACH DAY A NEW BEGINNING

Personal power can be defined as the ability to make certain choices and to live with their consequences. Finding this ability means discovering the difference between the choices we can make and the ones we cannot make. A simple fact of life is that there are things about the world and other people over which we have no power. Admitting and accepting our powerlessness focuses our attention on Self, the real source of our personal power.

Choices that may be well intentioned and made in a responsible manner do not always create the results we desire. Using the personal power we do have is still the most effective way to engage life's opportunities and challenges. Reacting to daily interactions and stimuli by making choices in accordance with our basic values manifests the outcomes we seek. Sometimes trying different ways to get what we need will eventually result in success. We may find more peace, however, by simply letting go of our attachment to the desired outcomes.

Exercising our power of choice can be perplexing because appropriate actions and responses are not defined or understood. Sometimes choices are simple, clear, and easy. At other times, they are complex, confusing, and difficult. Some circumstances call for us to use our power to make certain choices, while others do not. Due to this complexity, it is not surprising that our parents, teachers, and mentors have not been able to better prepare us to use our personal power.

We find personal power when we surrender the controlling misconception that others are in charge of us or that we are in charge of them. Letting go of this illusion frees us from an unworkable set of beliefs. Even when people try to meet their needs in violent, controlling, or abusive ways, we have the human right to use our personal power to take care of ourselves. Doing so in a loving manner is challenging and possible.

The search for Self reveals two simple tenets about power. **First, finding our power begins with acknowledging our powerlessness. Second, our real power is over Self.** Daily spiritual practice invites us to relish the choices that are ours to make and to let go of choices that are not. We have the power to choose our attitude, to be nurturing, or to layout a mission. We decide whether to hold on to things or release them, to take risks for growth, and to seek healing. Making loving choices to be more aware, sensitive, accepting, humble, open, trusting, and connected can transform our relationship with Self, as well as the world.

FIND
PERSONAL
POWER

Admit We Are Powerless

We are powerless over the outcome of all events involving us. And we are powerless over the lives of our friends and family members We are not powerless, however, over our own attitudes, our own behavior, our own self-image, our own determination, and our own commitment to life!
EACH DAY A NEW BEGINNING

The message many of us have received in our growth from childhood into adulthood is that we are in control of our lives. We start to believe we have more power than we actually do. This misunderstanding usually broadens to include the assumption that we are also responsible for changing other people and the events in their lives.

If things go well and we are happy, we assume we must be doing a good job managing and controlling our lives. If life is not good and we are not happy, then we think that things are not under control. We internalize messages that say when life is good, we are good, and when life is bad, so are we. **The assumption that we have more power than we do over the people and events in our lives is a mindset that is imposed upon us that could set us up for real or perceived failure.**

Just believing these messages does not make them true. Beliefs are not necessarily facts. Most beliefs are

FIND
PERSONAL
POWER

based on some truth but that doesn't make them completely true, useful, or reliable. Beliefs are concepts that we hold to be true or at least accurate enough for us to act upon. **Beliefs can be thought, taught, stated, shared, and imposed, but these human actions do not make a belief true.** The belief that we have certain power, whether true or not, still keeps us engaged in a struggle to use those powers. This challenge is a demanding, full-time job that stresses us to achieve an unrealistic and inaccurate goal. Exhaustion is a natural consequence of living our lives believing that we have more power than we actually do.

Unfortunately, people who have been trying to live up to their own unrealistic expectations and beliefs, or those of their children, spouses, partners, parents, siblings, neighbors, and co-workers, have missed one of the simple truths about Self. **We are powerless. There are people and events over which we have little or no choice, responsibility, or power.** We are not in control or even responsible for many things in life.

If we want to be free to find our personal power, we start by admitting our powerlessness. Then we can…

> …*stop blaming Self for failing to live according to unrealistic and inaccurate beliefs.*
>
> …*begin to forgive Self for believing that we are not good enough to live up to the expectations of others or the distorted expectations we hold for ourselves.*

...forgive Self for failing to do, say, act, and behave in the ways we assumed we should.

...turn over those things for which we have no control to a power greater than Self.

...begin to find real peace and personal power.

...start living in an authentic world of real love and integrity.

Admitting that there are things over which we have little or no power has created a fundamental shift in the lives of many people and has opened the door to seeing Self in a new, refreshing way. Exercising our ability to surrender is a spiritual practice that strengthens us in surprising ways that lead us further along the path to Self.

Adjust Our Attitude

It is in our attitude that we discover strength or weakness, hope or anxiety, determination or frustration. Alone, we determine whether our attitude will be loving or jaundiced. Today is mine to make. Let me choose my attitude with care.
THE PROMISE OF A NEW DAY

The attitude with which we approach life is a choice. We have the power to choose the position or perspective we will assume toward specific events and people in our lives. This orientation influences our actions and responses to the challenges we encounter each day. We can make the choice to frame our view of the world and its daily details positively and optimistically or negatively and pessimistically. **The challenge of life is certain; our choice of attitude is not.**

To hold a view of Self as a collection of flaws will decidedly ruin our day and happiness. Too often we fail to accept ourselves as imperfect human beings on a difficult path. Choosing our attitude is one area where we can enjoy real personal power. Amazingly, grumbling can turn into gratitude, arrows into gifts, and mistakes into learning when we adjust our attitude to positive instead of negative. **The attitude we choose determines whether**

FIND
PERSONAL
POWER

we scowl at each perceived flaw or welcome the challenge of the moment, prepared to transform even the toughest conflict into an opportunity for growth.

Our personal perspective of Self is strongly influenced by our choice of attitude. If we believe we are inadequate, unvalued failures, undeserving of joy and happiness, then this is the negative reality we can expect to manifest and experience. Alternatively, when we see Self as adequate, valued, and deserving, we are more likely to realize joy and fulfillment. Adopting a positive attitude in advance helps us weather life's storms.

Adequacy is a perception of our relative state of being. There are situations in life that cause us to experience a physical, mental, emotional, or spiritual sense of lacking. Ultimately, attitude can influence these perceptions of scarcity or abundance. So, we can choose between the perception of Self as not smart enough, not likeable or good enough to deserve love and happiness or we can see Self as intelligent, capable, and worthy of all the love and fulfillment we desire.

Rarely do we get to make all the choices regarding a situation; however, we invariably have an opportunity to play a role, make a contribution, or influence the outcome. Our attitude affects the quality of that contribution. We have the power to support our experiences and interactions by having an open, flexible, and loving attitude.

The search for Self is deep, and we may encounter painful secrets and what we perceive as ugly flaws. When we adjust our attitude to positive, we are more likely to look at these discoveries as healing revelations and beautiful gifts.

FIND
PERSONAL
POWER

Declare a Mission

We have the personal power to chart our course, to set our goals, and to take the necessary steps for their attainment. Imagining the person we strive to be, coupled with the clear details of the path we feel pulled to travel, is powerful preparation for the actual trip to our destination.
THE PROMISE OF A NEW DAY

Declaring our mission involves answering several basic questions. Who am I? Why am I here? How will I serve the world? What is my purpose in life, relationship, work, marriage, family, and community? How am I going to use the precious gifts of time and energy to fulfill my mission?

Our family, friends, teachers, spiritual leaders, coaches, and bosses are just some of the people who support and nurture us during very crucial times in our life. Most of us will be forever grateful for their time, attention, and their role in guiding us into the future.

However, they may unknowingly be usurping our personal power by attempting to write our life mission for us, rather than guiding us in declaring our own. They want us to be successful, productive, and happy; yet, some mentors attempt to compel us to do it their way. Maybe they don't trust us to figure it out on our own, or perhaps they need us to be successful for reasons of their own. No matter their motives, a portion of our life might be lived without a clear sense of who we are and why we are here.

Our personal power to answer our own questions about identity and purpose is lost if we are trying to live someone else's answers. If lucky, we may get more than one chance to look at our Self, life, and purpose from a place of personal freedom and maturity. This experience often becomes a transition point from the old us to the new us. Freedom from the imposed vision of others gives us the opportunity to declare our own mission in life.

We have all struggled with love and life and are hopefully much the wiser for our efforts. **A life mission based more on our own cumulative experience and wisdom can have more meaning than one based on the expectations of others.** If we are not happy with who we are or how we are living our lives today, our own deep passion and vision will guide us to a more appropriate declaration of Self and mission. We not only have the right but the responsibility to use our gifts to their fullest potential to help create the kind of world we want for Self, family, and community.

Seek Serenity

*Grant me the serenity to accept the things about myself that
I cannot change, the courage to change the one I can,
and the wisdom to know it is me.*
SERENITY MEDITATION FOR SELF

Serenity is a healthy state of being. When our lives are free from extreme highs and lows and their accompanying dis-stress and dis-ease, we experience the relative calm, freedom, and contentment of serenity. The simplicity of the serenity meditation helps us admit our powerlessness to be someone we are not and discover our personal power for living our daily lives relatively free from strain and pain.

Admitting our powerlessness to change the things we cannot change opens us to the possibility of finding the wisdom and courage to change the things we can about Self. Our personal power is our ability to make choices that allow for more serenity.

Serenity for Self involves internal and external surrender. Internal surrender happens as we are freed from the inappropriate expectations held by others and the distorted ones we hold for ourselves. Then, our perception of who we are and want to be can come into alignment with real Self. The gap between real and perceived Self slowly closes, relieving tension and fostering internal calm.

External surrender is the freedom that comes with letting go of our urge to control the people and events in our lives. When we stop fighting to exert power we do not have, a new era of more peaceful existence may be ours to enjoy.

Accepting our Self just as we are and forgiving Self for not being the person others say we are supposed-to-be create serenity. At first, it might seem like a miracle that our life does not come to an abrupt end as a result of accepting Self. Releasing the false perception that we are not good enough allows us to discover that we are lovable and valuable.

Huge relief often accompanies the realization of powerlessness. The hidden load that we carried masked its magnitude until the moment we actually set it down. We may have believed that no matter how heavy the load the cost of carrying this burden was in proportion to the benefit. However, letting go might be more beneficial than bearing the burden.

Serenity is like a magical elixir that soothes and rejuvenates us so we can let go, have courage, and find wisdom. Our lives might become more peaceful and less stressful if we try to be more serene beings. Serenity can happen as we learn to accept Self just the way we are.

Laugh a Lot

Does laughter have healing power? Healing isn't the word.
Therapeutic, maybe, or cathartic. After being in extreme
situations, it kind of brings you back to life.
ROBIN WILLIAMS

Life is full of joy and suffering. Having a sense of humor acknowledges happy times in life and helps us survive the painful ones. **Laughter is a natural and pleasurable way to allow positive, joyful energy to flow throughout our bodies.** This spontaneous release provides some relief, even in the midst of the most desperate times, and balances the inevitable, ill effects of loss and grief.

Not an entirely enjoyable trip, our inward journey could be compared to open-heart surgery. The deeper we descend, the more we may connect with old pain or hidden feelings. We can carry humor with us as a form of portable first-aid, to soothe and heal the pain that conceals some of these valuable gifts. Laughter displaces the shadows and lightens up the dark places.

In his book *Anatomy of an Illness*, Norman Cousins shared how he relied on laughter to overcome his life-threatening illness. There is some evidence that laughter can actually increase the levels of certain desirable chemicals in our brain and body. Throughout human history, humor and laughter have demonstrated the ability to work wonders on mind, body, and spirit.

Remembering to bring fun and play into every aspect of life can be a loving and nurturing choice, whether we are making silly faces with a child or exchanging intellectual banter with adults. Joyful activities help us relax and de-stress, strengthen our connection to Self, and form loving bonds with others. **Humor and laughter are signs of a positive, resilient attitude, and using them frequently reflects the personal choice to view Self and the world with acceptance and forgiveness.**

As mature adults, we are often called on to be responsible and deal with important issues. However, taking Self or our duties too seriously can cost us our emotional and spiritual flexibility. Nervous laughter may not be a product of real joy; instead, it could be used to hide fear or shame. Using humor to sidestep reality or distract us from the gravity of a situation may also be unhealthy and inappropriate. Finding the right balance between fun and focus reflects wisdom that comes with awareness, age, and experience.

There are situations when humor and laughter are not beneficial. Ridiculing Self to gain false acceptance into a group is not being true to ourselves or to those with whom we wish to connect. Humor can be detrimental when we seek to take pleasure at the expense of others. This choice demeans them as well as us.

In sharp contrast, good-hearted humor serves to bind us powerfully to others, while strengthening our internal, spiritual connection to Self. In most situations good-natured laughter, like a smile, expresses universal friendship and goodwill that can open more boundaries and borders than any passport.

We have the power to dance or drag our Self through life. Letting the joyful power of laughter flow often and freely nurtures us in wonderful ways. **Our spontaneous and energetic expression of joy through laughter reminds us that our greatest purpose in life and relationship is to love and be loved.**

FIND
PERSONAL
POWER

Let Go

Letting go is a process. You have to know when to apply it,
what to let go of, and how to let go. Letting go releases
you from this insistent grip, and when you let go,
new forms of reality can enter.
DEEPAK CHOPRA

Clinging to old beliefs, behaviors, and ideas is a common human characteristic. We usually do so because we derive some assurance, a sense of safety, security, or some payoff from this choice. Holding on can limit our power to pursue new possibilities in the present moment.

Throughout life we receive less than loving and nurturing messages from many sources. From this information we make assumptions that influence our view of Self. **Believing and holding tightly to negative assumptions that we are not smart enough, not physically attractive enough, or not good enough are some of the harmful choices that we make.** These internalized perceptions, whether accurate or not, influence what we say or do in order to be seen, heard, valued, and loved. **This erroneous information can become a negative belief system that we carry within us until we make the choices to change.**

Maintaining an illusion of false power is another example of not letting go. Attempting to control those things over which we have little or no real power frustrates us, especially when our efforts fail to produce the results we need. Refusing to let go keeps us stuck and prevents beneficial change and growth.

Letting go is a process that involves courage and risk. This process might be as simple as releasing old beliefs and assumptions or as difficult as intensive therapy and counseling. Identifying the personal reasons for holding on to old stuff plays a crucial role in letting go. These discoveries may include unfinished emotional or spiritual business that has never been resolved or forgiveness issues that continue to haunt us.

Sometimes letting go means detaching from the problem and doing nothing at all. **Choosing to take no action can allow our emotional turbulence to calm, empowering us to accept things as they are or to see them differently.** Ultimately, letting go creates more inner peace and takes less energy than holding on.

Letting go is initially accompanied by a huge sigh of relief, and our life becomes lighter, easier, and freer. This newfound freedom clears the way for us to make new choices about our boundaries, commitments, feelings, and reactions. Letting go opens wide the path to Self, allows us to trust in a power greater than Self, connects us to others in loving ways, and honors the ability of other people to take care of themselves.

Risk Growth

*My hardest lessons are the ones I resist the most. But, when
all is said and done, I see those same lessons have
also taught me the most.*

PAUL FERRINI

Growth is choice. When we strive to engage Self
and others in healthy relationship, we grow.
This positive change occurs when we make loving choices
in real time, especially in our relationship with Self. We
have the personal power to make many choices that
nurture our physical, emotional, mental, and spiritual
development.

Resisting growth is also a choice, often our first. Many
of us consider ourselves to be courageous adventurers in
life, committed to exploring and learning about Self and
other people. Yet, we consciously or unconsciously make
less than loving and nurturing choices that allow the
opportunities for growth to pass. Acquiring information
and knowledge about how to grow can be relatively easy.
The hard part is applying it in our everyday lives, especially
when the growing involves Self.

**Growth is beneficial change and change is a natural,
inevitable part of life.** The choice to invite change can be
scary, disruptive, and painful, even when the growth is

positive and constructive. Many of us consider ourselves safe, secure, and satisfied with our life and relationships; therefore, choosing to change is not necessarily desirable or easy. **The growth process brings us face to face with our fears, especially the fear of separation from the familiar and comfortable.** Fear tempts us to resist change or avoid it altogether, postponing or preventing new experiences. Making loving and nurturing choices, while acknowledging and owning our fears, empowers us to embrace change and enjoy the rewards of growth.

Growth is risky. Most people would prefer to experience joy and fulfillment without taking risks and possible discomfort. We cannot make room for what is new without letting go of the old. Releasing causes a sense of loss, usually accompanied by sadness and fear, even when we are replacing old suffering with newfound joy. People are motivated to take risks because they seek a greater return or payoff. Ultimately, the payoff for risking growth in relationships is to love and be loved more.

Growth is a conscious choice to risk the inward journey into the yet unexplored territory of Self. Having the courage to venture into these new areas inevitably deepens our relationship to Self and helps us realize our full potential.

Tend Spiritual Flames

Flickering candles
We're spiritual beings
On a human path.
VICTOR LaCERVA, M.D.

Despite a wide variety of personal beliefs concerning the nature of spirit, many people are open to the possibility that the human body serves as a vessel for some form of energy. There is little question that a living body is filled with life energy, while it is obviously absent from a lifeless one. For the purpose of our work, this life energy will be called spiritual energy.

The origin of spiritual energy is a mystery, and its exact nature has so far defied general consensus. **While the ever-expanding theological and scientific search for answers continues, its progress supports the possibility that spiritual energy exists and profoundly impacts our lives and relationships.** Whatever a person's belief about spiritual energy, using the flame of a flickering candle as a metaphor for understanding our ability to nurture or diminish Self will hopefully prove useful.

When we tend the flickering flame of our spiritual energy, the light shines brightly to the external world. **We nurture our spiritual energy by making conscious choices to behave and think in alignment with the** person we are and the person we want to become. Our capacity to love and care for Self, to be aware of the effects of our choices, and to live life with compassion and respect instead of in anger and judgment are ways we tend our flickering flame.

When denied the ingredients for a rich, bright flame, our spiritual energy is neglected and wanes. We appear dark and negative to others because there is an absence of love, respect, compassion, and other qualities that are essential to healthy interactions. Our ability to heal and grow Self is diminished, and the possibilities for creating and sharing meaningful relationships are limited. **How we nurture our spiritual energy can influence our human characteristics and the life experiences we create.**

The degree to which our spiritual energy fills us and can shine into the world depends on our skill to tend our own inner flame. Its light illuminates that which is greater than Self, those who are the same as Self, and the one who is Self.

Learn to Love Self

Love is the will to extend one's self for the purpose of
nurturing one's own or another's spiritual growth.
SCOTT PECK

We have the power to love Self. Because many of the lessons and messages acquired along our life path have been less than loving and nurturing, many of us have had to learn new ways to love Self. Hopefully, this book brings to light many parts of Self we have forgotten or never noticed. Reading, studying, and trying to apply wisdom, some of which is very old and some of which is very new, are nurturing choices that acknowledge and deepen our relationship with Self.

Loving ourselves can be the key to knowing and healing Self. Our loving relationship with Self becomes the model for our loving relationship with others. Healing our Self makes us whole and helps us become a source of healing for others. Living and relating as a loving Self can be, in turn, the key to loving, knowing, and appreciating others.

A misconception assumes love of Self demonstrates selfish, egocentric, or narcissistic behavior. These forms of self-orientation are usually unhealthy attempts to compensate for perceived inadequacies and involve an exclusive focus on Self that is detrimental to others. Healthy love of Self, on the other hand, enhances love for others.

Love is the birthright of every human being. Finding personal power to make choices, especially the one to love Self, satisfies our innate human need to be loved and helps us find the serenity we seek. Learning to love Self helps us heal and grow into whole, healthy human beings who become sources of loving energy for the world.

Use Personal Power to Change the World

Each time a man stands up for an ideal, or acts to improve the lot of others, or strikes out against injustice, he sends forth a tiny ripple of hope, and crossing each other from a million different centers of energy and daring, those ripples build a current that can sweep down the mightiest walls of oppression and resistance.

ROBERT F. KENNEDY

G lancing at the morning headlines can be a painful experience for many of us. The news is often populated with stories about war, murder, violence, and other destructive choices people rely on to solve their problems. There may always be some form of negative conflict in the world and a press of others who want to tell us about it. Despite our unwillingness to look at these painful events, they generate real consequences that we must bear.

While there are different reactions to this daily barrage of strife and fear in the news, anger and frustration are two that are frequently directed at some of the people in these stories. Some people want to rail at the system and the societal conditions that cause these dilemmas, while others just want to avoid dealing with these realities, no matter how close or distant. Most of us feel powerless to

FIND
PERSONAL
POWER

do anything about these community or global issues. Are we really powerless to fix the problems?

We have discovered that there are many things over which we have no power or choice. Accepting our power-lessness makes us more aware of the things over which we do have power. Assuming that we want some of the problems solved even though we are powerless to fix them directly, what can we do to promote positive change in our world?

We can use our power to act and react in healthy, constructive ways as opportunities appear in our daily interaction with Self and others. Showing more love, compassion, acceptance, and forgiveness in our own personal lives makes a positive difference. M.K. Gandhi said, "Be the change you wish to see." The cumulative effect of these small, positive, personal choices is what ultimately determines the quality of the relationships in any community. Whether it is our local or global neighborhood, more loving and nurturing behavior con-tributes to the shift towards the world we wish to see.

Although limited, our personal power over our own lives, actions, and reactions may be all that we need to make a positive difference. We can use our personal power to bring more love into our life, promoting whole-ness and well-being. As a whole, more satisfied, joyful Self, we now become love-generating power centers that radiate loving and nurturing energy into our families, groups, and communities. This powerful, healing force affects every single action and reaction in which we are involved. The collective strength of this energy ripples throughout our lives, homes, neighborhoods, workplaces, cities, regions, cultures, countries, and even the world, stimulating change one loving act at a time.

The rest of this book is about the choices we can make that will consciously acknowledge and support Self as we continue the inward journey. What we learn about love and its ability to heal will take us to the very center of Self. The path we follow on our journey seeking Self is the same one we walk on our journey to love and heal others.

FIND
PERSONAL
POWER

WAY 3

DISCOVER FEELINGS

But if you can feel your emotions, you are not far from the radiant inner body just underneath. If you are mainly in your head, the distance is much greater, and you need to bring consciousness into the emotional body before you can reach the inner body.

ECKHART TOLLE

Melting My Stone

Martin Prechtel, a Mayan shaman and healer, calls sorrow that has never been tearfully expressed as *Shahabishokaba*, or petrified sorrow. The transformation of a vibrant, healthy heart into a mass of stone is an imperceptible process that takes a long time, and that is exactly what happened to mine.

One day, as I sat in my therapist's office reflecting on the emotional paralysis that characterized my life at that time, I realized that my heart had turned to stone. My wonderful counselor took me through a gentle process that changed my ability to feel. She asked me to close my eyes and take a good, close look at my heart, something I had not done in my forty-plus years. My focused intrusion on the middle of my chest stirred a deep, intense sadness. Shock overcame surprise as I discovered a cold, hard stone where once my warm, compassionate heart had been. For me, this process began early in life.

As a child, I enjoyed much privilege, laughter, and joy, and I experienced a full range of emotions in my little boy body. Like many children, I also endured less than loving and nurturing events, messages, and actions from loved ones trying to parent, teach, or guide my growth and development. Many of the wounds that occurred in my youth were unintentional and may have been motivated by love. In any case, I took these hurts more deeply to heart than I realized at the time, forming beliefs and making decisions that unknowingly turned my heart to stone.

For years I dishonored my feelings and steadily honed my skills at minimizing my pain and suffering. My childhood anger, once fast and fleeting, became progressively more furious and lasting, and the arrows I encountered in life embedded deeply into my body. The shaming words, unkind comments, humiliating face slaps, and family suicides stung deeply and lingered in my memory, convincing me that feelings were bad and something I wanted to avoid.

As the years passed, my family and the outside world were less willing to witness my feelings so I began to stuff, medicate, and shut down my emotions. For over 20 years I was under the illusion that these techniques were working. Slowly, these methods became less and less effective at relieving my suffering, and I found myself in the dark days before my surrender. Finally, when I had no other tricks up my sleeve, I had to face personal destruction, disaster, and death before I was willing to relinquish my old ways and consider the possibility of new choices. Only then did I open up and see my life and experience my feelings differently. Only then did change come.

So, on that fateful day and with the guidance of a gentle healer, I imagined tenderly holding my heart like a baby, loving and healing it into the feeling heart I wanted it to become. Recovery and growth have slowly softened and transformed my heart into a source of love and compassion. I have even learned to cry and grieve. Today, I am more authentically and intimately connected to my Self and my family than ever. I spend special time with my men's group, 12-step meetings, and I participate in other safe, healing circles where my feelings are welcome. My inner journey continues, one feeling at a time.

DISCOVER
FEELINGS

Discover Feelings

The journey into the sensate self offers a pathway to recover
our trust in our body and its wisdom.
WENDY PALMER

As we proceed on our search for Self, many fascinating, new discoveries about who we are and how we work will come to light. Leo Buscalia, a professor of education, inspiring author, and enthusiastic lecturer, described the process of personal development and becoming the Self you were meant to be as the art of being fully human. This learning process brings us face to face with one of the most intriguing attributes of being fully human, the phenomena called feelings.

Why is discovering our feelings important, when we already know they exist within us? Because our feelings, although obvious, are frequently ignored, suppressed or inhibited in our modern, so-called civilized life styles. As we grow up, our thinking, rational Self can become separated from our feeling, intuitive Self. If this happens, one of our greatest human qualities, the ability to experience the full range of emotional energy, can be slowly and imperceptibly lost. Discovering our feelings anew helps us reunite our head and our body to create a whole Self.

We experience feelings every moment we are alive. Awake or asleep, our body is pulsing with waves of emotional energy that well up and move through and out of us. Our feelings are an integral and natural part of who we are, whether we notice them or not. Most of us assume our brain's sole function is to support our thinking Self. In fact, our brain spends as much, if not more, time sensing and utilizing the incredible amount of emotional and spiritual energy that makes up our feeling Self.

Emotional literacy implies we are aware of our feeling experiences and understand their meaning. The more familiar we are with our feelings, the more connected we become with our emotional nature, even when the experience is not comfortable. Too often feelings are treated like uninvited strangers that show up at our front door, only to be allowed entrance in spite of initial distrust. With distracted attention, these unwanted visitors are reluctantly entertained and quickly dismissed. Unknowingly, their precious gifts can be ignored and lost.

Our experience of feelings can range from blissful to painful. For many of us, they can be awkward and uncomfortable, making them difficult to get to know. Maybe that is why we sometimes avoid, suppress, inhibit, and dishonor their presence. Consciously honoring our feelings promotes healthy relationship with Self and other people. **Originating from deep within, feelings reflect our innermost workings and lead us down pathways to the real origins of behavior. Feelings help**

us comprehend why we do what we do. Those that are denied or suppressed in the moment are the most difficult to uncover later and take the most personal work to fully experience.

We can spend an entire lifetime trying to understand these remarkable, elusive happenings called feelings. Our physical, emotional, mental, and spiritual energies come together in unknown ways to form this unpredictable human weather, whose temperamental changes can fill us with the well-being of a gorgeous, sunny day or wrack us with the anger of a volatile thunderstorm. These powerful forces can render us asunder or nurture us with healing and closure. Amazing and mysterious, feelings are gifts that express our individuality and simultaneously bind us to the other members of the Greater Human Family.

Getting to know our emotions and delving into their mysteries deepen our quest for Self and tap the very source of our excitement and compassion. The external manifestations of feelings are behaviors, and each emotion marks a doorway to the inner Self. **Refusing to open these portals to our hidden emotions imprisons their energy and ensures that our woundedness will be lived out in our words, thoughts, and deeds.** Without discovering and celebrating the significance of our feelings, we cannot link the cause of our behavior with the effect of our anger, sadness, joy, fear, and shame. Cultivating intimacy with our feelings, asking questions about our observable behaviors, and exploring our shadows provide the vital information we need for authentic healing and growth.

Experience Feelings Fully in the Moment

Give your fullest attention to whatever the moment presents.
This implies that you also completely accept what is,
because you cannot give your full attention to
something and at the same time resist it.
ECKHART TOLLE

Feelings are a splendid, healing gift we share as human beings. Experiencing our feelings fully in the moment means listening to and honoring them, even the painful ones, the very instant they arise. Our ability to do so is central to health and relationship.

Although making friends with our feelings has rewards, acknowledging them is a daunting challenge. Giving attention to activities that we enjoy is easy. Not surprisingly though, many of us find it difficult to spend time with some of our feelings, preferring to direct our attention to making friends with work, food, sex, television, sports, gambling, risk-taking, alcohol, drugs, and other forms of distraction. There may be an immediate, substantial pay-off for this type of evasive behavior. **Choices that inhibit our feelings may create temporary relief in the moment but could carry the longer-term, detrimental effects of suffering, rejection, or abandonment.**

DISCOVER
FEELINGS

Our technologically advanced and economically sophisticated culture has a dampening effect on the full expression of emotions. We come by our aversion to feelings honestly. **Dishonoring feelings has been modeled and witnessed by countless generations of families, communities, societies, and cultures that have not allowed the full, in-the-moment expression of all feelings. We have been literally and culturally taught to dishonor a significant portion of our range of emotional experiences.** This suppression negates our humanness and blocks the path to Self.

For instance, in many modern western cultures, men are discouraged from displaying feelings of sadness or fear, because these feelings are considered unmanly and thought to reveal character weakness. In a similar fashion, women are discouraged from overtly exhibiting their anger or behaving in ways that might appear unladylike. In these examples, we have been culturally programmed to believe that experiencing some of our feelings fully in the moment is not acceptable. Criticism, teasing, ridiculing, and being ostracized by peers or family are powerful deterrents from experiencing our feelings fully and completely.

Developing an appreciation and awareness that our feelings play an essential role in our inner journey to healthy relationship can counterbalance these prevailing, cultural trends and the resulting problems fostered in our society. **Feelings are crucial indicators that we** are fully alive and engaged, and they are integral to our wholeness. Repressing our feelings by blocking or stuffing them damages our personal health and has been directly linked to dysfunctional human behavior and interaction. Inhibiting them changes us and alters how we function as physiological and spiritual beings.

Ocean waves need a vast sea of space in which to move back and forth, building and releasing their energy. Waves become destructive when they encounter man-made barriers that impede the flow of their energy. So do the waves of emotional energy that surge through us. Any attempt to inhibit the ebb and flow of feelings causes a destructive accumulation of energy that eventually leads to a loss of emotional center and balance.

The range of our emotional experience shrinks if we inhibit feelings, while the expression of the remaining emotions may actually accumulate and intensify. This built-up, emotional energy seeks to be released, perhaps even violently, and can be triggered by a minor, non-related event or action. Displays of disproportionate emotional outbursts, like rage, uncontrollable sobbing, or inappropriate laughter, may be evidence of limited and intensified emotions.

Stuffing or restricting our feelings produces internal wounds that can be covered up by our day-to-day living experiences. If these wounds and the feelings associated with them are not honored, they fester and create longer-term problems for us that wait to be addressed in our relationships. Unfortunately, they do not just go away. Big feelings that happen around small issues can be a sign of unexperienced, unresolved, or unhealed feelings and wounds. We would not ignore someone who was crying out in need or pain. Why, then, would we ignore our own feelings when they cry out for attention?

Feelings that are experienced fully in the moment promote good health and wholeness. The more we are able to notice and allow our feelings, the less we will be burdened by the baggage of stuffed feelings and the toxic effects that their trapped energy can have on our lives and relationships. If we give our feelings only partial attention, some of their value and meaning can be lost. The conscious practice of bringing all that is happening within us, especially our feelings, fully into each moment makes it possible for us to reap the complete benefits of our human experiences.

Stop Inhibiting Feelings

We need the information that comes from our emotions in order to take care of ourselves properly. We need to be in touch with our emotions, acknowledging them, listening to them, and being able to express them and communicate them when we choose.
PHILIP ROGERS

Every day we experience numerous feelings that we choose to either inhibit or honor. This conscious or unconscious choice to inhibit a feeling can have a profound effect on our personal growth.

Human feelings are complex, physiological processes that involve many steps, any of which can easily be disrupted or blocked. **The purpose of our feelings is to communicate information about our state of being.** This information is sometimes clear, while at other times more subtle and difficult to discern. If we fail to seize the initial opportunity to consciously allow the fulfillment of the complete feeling process, the intended messages could be missed.

We humans tend to avoid pain and seek comfort. This behavior does not serve us well when it inhibits feelings. With the dexterity of a magician's sleight of hand, we are able to distract our mind and, by doing so, avoid coming face-to-face with our feelings. We trick our Self into *thinking* rather than *feeling* the emotional content of our experiences. Inhibiting our feelings becomes a skill that we quickly and unconsciously employ whenever painful or uncomfortable emotional energy arises within our mind, heart, and body.

These magic-like tricks can be conjured up in a variety of ways and become behavioral patterns that provide temporary relief from suffering by interfering with our normal feeling process. These skills for not experiencing our feelings fully in the moment can be learned from role models and relationships. We can even interfere with the process before it begins or after it has ended.

Becoming aware of these patterns that inhibit our feelings is the next step on the path to seeking Self. Consider the following skillful choices that inhibit feelings.

Avoiding

Avoiding involves simply moving away from an approaching feeling that appears scary, displeasing, or

uncomfortable. Suddenly changing the subject, diverting our attention, or refusing to dwell on a past memory are examples of making conscious choices or taking unconscious action not to connect with our feelings. Any diversion, no matter how small, may incur costs greater than we might realize.

Giving feelings away is another method to avoid them. Blaming others for how we feel or disclosing our feelings as though they belonged to someone else are two very common tricks we use to give our feelings away.

Interrupting

We can't always see our feelings coming in time to avoid them, so another way to inhibit them is to interrupt the process. Feelings well up naturally, often at inopportune times. Unlike avoidance, feelings we interrupt have somehow already started or begun. When unwanted feelings come up, it is possible to consciously or unconsciously stop the natural flow of their emotional energy.

Minimizing

Minimizing is any mental judgment, rationalization, or qualification of a feeling that detracts from its impact and real meaning. We either feel a certain feeling or we don't. One example of minimizing is when the intensity of a feeling becomes more significant than the message that the feeling is trying to convey. Characterizing our emotional state as being a *little* upset, *slightly* nervous, or *kind of* disappointed downplays the *mad, sad, glad,* or *afraid* feeling experiences and diminishes their significance. Owning our anger, fear, shame, or joy clarifies the feeling and its meaning.

Sometimes using certain words to name our emotional experiences reduces our awareness of the actual feeling. Although accurate and perhaps more pleasing to the ear, these words minimize our connection to an emotional experience rather than maximize it. For instance, when we describe ourselves as blah, gloomy, or blue, we may not get that we are sad. Likewise, are we just plain angry when we use the words frustrated or irritated to describe how we feel? If we are having trouble connecting with our emotional experiences, the use of certain words can make our feelings less clear, while others can be used to make a much stronger connection to the main emotional experience.

Stuffing

Another very common way to prevent our feelings from being experienced in the moment is to stuff them away before fully experiencing and expressing them. Sometimes we shove our feelings down into our bodies just as they start to well up.

Perhaps we stifle the urge to speak or exhibit feelings of anger, sadness, or happiness because we believe expressing our feelings openly would compromise our value or keep us from being loved. Often, we keep our feelings inside because we do not want to appear vulnerable or weak. The anticipation of a negative reaction inhibits the external expression of our feelings, and we choose behavior that sidesteps a possible undesirable consequence.

Stuffing is potentially one of the most harmful ways to inhibit our feelings because it traps the emotional energy of the feeling in our body. The physiological changes and the associated negative energy of stuffed feelings remain unresolved within us, undermining our sense of well-being and distracting us out of the present moment. Stuffing feelings is a dysfunctional process considered by many to be a major source of stress, serious dis-ease, and illness.

Intellectualizing

Babies and children experience and express their feelings effortlessly. This freedom can be lost or emphatically discouraged by caretakers, and this may explain why we come to believe that it is more prudent to control our feelings. Separation of our feeling Self from our thinking Self is not a natural requirement for growing up; however, many people learn to make this choice for protection or to please others.

When we experience feelings, emotional energy flushes through our entire body. Our heart starts pounding; our breathing becomes labored; our stomach begins to spasm; our palms sweat; and our muscles tense. The silent significance of our feelings stimulates this myriad of physical responses to what is happening within us.

Facial expressions, hair standing on end, and headaches are some of the non-thinking reactions to feelings that happen in our heads. This mental function of feelings can trigger a variety of thoughts, beliefs, and assumptions.

The disconnection of the heart from the head happens when the thinking part of the process blocks, shuts down, or inhibits the feeling experience.

By intellectualizing our feelings, we dilute them and delude ourselves. Thinking and explaining away any part of our feelings may cause the physical sensations to decrease or even cease, and our chance to experience our feelings fully in the moment can be lost. By giving our painful experiences the full attention and participation they deserve, we can resist the temptation to make clever explanations.

Medicating

Medicating is a term that usually refers to the use of medicine to treat illness. In the world of addiction the word medicating is commonly used to describe certain behaviors, including the consumption of drugs and substances, that mask or cover our feelings. Here, medicating refers to the pain-killing attributes of certain behaviors that may provide relief by inhibiting undesired feelings. The relief is only temporary because the discomfort is suppressed and delayed rather than permanently alleviated. Many people have been deeply wounded from less than loving and nurturing experiences and, without realizing it, have resorted to medicating their painful feelings.

People find many different behaviors that medicate away these states of suffering and dis-ease, including smoking, drinking, drugging, and overeating. More socially acceptable, even admired, behaviors can be used to mask our feelings. Work, service, religion, and even play can be pursued in ways that are really a means of inhibiting feelings. Other innocuous behaviors that may be used to medicate our feelings include over-indulging in television, movies, sports, sex, excitement, cleanliness, perfection, neatness, and even talking.

When we medicate our feelings away rather than work our way through them, we risk becoming stuck emotionally. If our emotional development and growth are arrested, we are denied the value of fully embracing emotional experiences from beginning to end.

Substituting

Another unconscious way we inhibit feelings involves substituting one feeling experience for another. For example, when some people feel fearful or sad, they may display gladness by laughing or giggling. We may be substituting when the internal feeling experience does not match our external words and actions. Real feelings are hidden from our Self and others when we replace one feeling with another.

In summary, inhibiting feelings robs us of important information and insight about our inner Self, and their blocked energy remains in us, impatiently awaiting release. Each missed opportunity prevents us from being a natural, feeling human being. **Feelings are a miracle of human nature and hold in their message the gift of our anger, sadness, joy, and fear.**

Honor Feelings

The only way out is through!
FRITZ PERLS

Honoring our feelings means to experience them fully and appropriately in the moment. The ideal of honor implies respect, reverence, honesty, and authenticity, qualities that offer guidance as we seek to embrace our feelings. Failing to acknowledge and accept our feelings dishonors one of our most valuable human attributes.

Learning to welcome feelings as we would good friends can transform old fears into new, hopeful experiences. **Honored feelings give us insight about our needs and behaviors.** Although sometimes painful, this knowledge enlightens and empowers us. Following are some of the ways we honor feelings by making choices that celebrate rather than inhibit their full experience and meaning.

Notice Our Feelings

Each day is filled with flurries of activity. Our head is occupied with thousands of thoughts and our heart is congested with a rush of many emerging feelings. Even if we are mindful and aware, distractions abound and our feelings can easily go unnoticed.

Arising from an internal wellspring of deeper emotional energy, feelings will be noticed when we pay closer attention to the inner happenings and sensations of our body and consciously seek to spot them. Just noticing that we are having a feeling experience is the beginning of honoring their existence and relevance.

Own Our Feelings

If there is one thing we could call our very own in this life, it would be our feelings. Their energy, sensations and meaning all originate within our bodies and belong exclusively to us. Giving away our feelings is not a healthy option. So, why not take full ownership?

Taking full responsibility for our feelings keeps us on a true path to Self. A simple but powerful tool for owning them is to start using I-statements when we are talking about feelings. Making statements, like *I feel mad*, *I feel sad*, *I feel glad*, or *I feel afraid*, help us own our feelings completely, their sensations, messages, and origin.

Name Our Feelings

If we want to get to know people, we ask their name, socialize with them, and become familiar with their history and personality. Using their names honors them by acknowledging their presence.

Similarly, our feelings can be honored and validated if we call them by name in the moment they arise. Although many words can be used to describe feelings, using the five primary names is a helpful way to connect a sensation to the actual emotional experiences of *mad, sad, glad, afraid,* and *ashamed.*

Stop Medicating Our Feelings

Non-doctor prescribed medicating, the use of certain behaviors to mask our feelings, offers many people temporary freedom from pain, but it dishonors feelings while simulating an illusion of well-being. The medicating effects of certain substances or activities usually wear off quickly, escalating our drive to medicate again and trapping us in a potentially addictive downward spiral with undesirable consequences. **This type of medicating disconnects us from our real feelings, and we miss the opportunity to be more fully human, to be vulnerable, to be wounded, to heal, and to grow.**

We start honoring our feelings when we stop medicating. The potential for new beginnings is created, opening a door on our path of personal and emotional growth.

Special Note: Medicating is the tip of a very large iceberg. Freeing ourselves from medicating, codependent, obsessive-compulsive behaviors and addictions is not easy. Just saying "no" usually does not work. If you think you have a problem with medicating, especially addictive behaviors, and you want more information, see the list of web resources at the back of the book.

Allow Feelings to Happen

Even when we slow down, notice, acknowledge, and name our feelings, it is easy to rush them and interfere with their natural expression. The temptation to jump out of the feeling experience and into a head experience is strong. Surrendering to feelings instead of minimizing, stuffing, or interrupting them allows emotions to be fully experienced in the moment, resulting in growth, healing, and a rich life.

Let anger come and go. Anger is an emotion that comes up fairly easily for most people. Even so, suppressed anger is one of the root causes of physical and verbal violence in our world. The problem occurs when we allow angry emotions to come out in ways that do more harm than good. Like crying, expressing anger can ultimately be a purging experience. **If we fail to release our angry energy through some clearing process, we set ourselves up for an inevitable release of pent-up, emotional energy, which can be toxic and destructive to our relationships.**

Allowing anger to arise and be expressed in non-destructive ways is essential for health. Much of the danger and destructiveness we associate with anger is actually the result of suppressed or stuffed anger being released rapidly and inappropriately. **All feelings are okay; all behaviors are not.**

Our angry energy often blocks our view of deeper, inner issues, which can only be seen and addressed once the angry energy that has been obscuring them has been released. It has been said that we have a mountain of anger that covers a lake of sadness.

Finding safe ways to express our anger makes it possible for us to experience its burning flush without any damaging effects as it moves completely through us. Experiencing anger appropriately leaves us renewed, calm, and clear.

Sit With Our Sadness. Sadness is a feeling that arises when we experience loss, usually the loss of love. Many of us resist our sad feelings because they are uncomfortable and painful. The more completely we embrace our sadness, the more we are able to grieve our loss and its significance in our lives. Rather than avoid sadness, we could choose to hold it, sit with it, wallow in it, grieve deeply, and surrender completely when it calls. This, combined with crying, helps relieve the unavoidable pain and suffering that is an integral part of being alive and caring about others.

Sadness may be triggered by a sudden event, but it cannot be rushed. The time to grieve properly and to heal can be lengthy. No matter how long our grieving lasts, complete recovery is sometimes never finished. **Sitting with our sadness involves dealing with the pain numerous times before we are ready to let it go and reach closure.**

Relieving the pain of sadness works best when our tears flow. While some women are already pretty good at this one, many men find crying an especially difficult way to allow their sad emotions. **Not only is it okay for men to be sad and to cry, it is essential.** The world suffers the consequences of men's un-cried tears and suppressed sadness. No matter how great the pain or suffering, a good cry is a natural way of healing. No one has to bear inevitable suffering in silent, dry pain.

Face our Fears. The best way to overcome our fears is to allow and honor these feelings. Fear is frequently fostered by a lack of knowledge and understanding that feeds on itself and can keep us in a dark, endless cycle of dysfunction and despair. Fearful feelings are scary and uncomfortable; and anger, withdrawal, and stress are often used to avoid and disguise our feelings of fear. Acknowledging and embracing our emotional experiences expose our underlying fears so that we can face them.

Many fears are uncovered on our search for Self. One of the most revealing is the fear of not being loved. Many of us believe that we are not good enough and fear rejection or isolation from our families, friends, or social groups. Allowing our most uncomfortable feelings brings light and love into the darkness of our life, dissolving the binding effects of our fears. Honoring our fears gives us a chance to find reassurance and safety.

Laissez les bon tempes roulez! Let the good times roll naturally. We all have our own way of being happy and enjoying ourselves. As long as we are not doing so at the expense of others, expressing our joy and celebrating life honors our glad feelings.

Feeling joy and happiness is fairly easy for most of us, but there are some people who lose their ability to do so because of the unresolved grief, anger and unhealed wounds they carry. Happiness is available to all who have the courage and the desire to pursue the search for Self. On this inner journey, we discover the causes of our unhappiness and sources for more joy.

Confusing happiness with medicating is also fairly common. Celebrating does not require medicating behaviors so seek to experience joy and happiness naturally. Allowing our joy and happiness does not always have to take the form of riotous partying. Most of our glad feelings come in small daily doses, as we learn to accept with gratitude all of life's simple wonders, pleasures, and gifts.

Respect Our Feelings

Although a miracle of divine design, feelings are an integral part of life, and their natural function is essential for health. Too often, we treat our feelings like inconvenient intruders, and our lack of appreciation for these good friends fosters an attitude of contempt, rather than the awe and respect they deserve. Choosing a respectful attitude toward emotional experiences celebrates our human uniqueness and sensitivity.

Listen To and Understand Our Feelings

Feelings are messengers that convey information about our inner dynamics. Listening to our feelings exposes our needs, the triggers for our behaviors. Joy communicates happiness and contentment. Cacophonous anger demands satisfaction. Sadness or shame mourns loss or unfulfilled potential. Our many feelings alert us to unmet needs that require attention or to some choice we have yet to make.

Fear, frustration, and confusion accompany feelings we do not understand. We can better comprehend why feelings are happening if we listen carefully for their message and experience them fully in the moment. Listening and understanding promote knowledge of Self and empower us to make informed choices that honor our feelings and fulfill our needs.

Share Our Feelings

A really wonderful way to acknowledge and make sense of what is going on inside of us is to share our feelings with someone else. Having a friend, a family member, or community group that is willing to listen and suspend judgment while we describe our emotional experiences openly and honestly honors our feelings.

Accept Our Feelings

Acceptance marks the beginning of the end of our struggle to avoid, ignore, minimize, intellectualize, and medicate feelings. With acceptance, we begin owning our feelings as an integral part of Self and stop the tricks that separate us from our emotions. When we embrace our emotional experiences, the barriers separating all of our parts dissolve, and we become a whole, integrated Self.

Feelings are a gift. They are neither good or bad nor right or wrong. They just are. They arise spontaneously and authentically to give us a richer, fuller life, if we allow them to happen. We heal and grow when we choose to honor our feelings.

133

Call Feelings by Name

By developing a vocabulary of feelings that allows us to clearly and specifically name or identify our emotions, we can connect more easily with one another.

MARSHALL B. ROSENBERG

Noticing and calling our feelings by name is a simple way of claiming them and healing Self. Because feelings can irrefutably arise in the emotional heat of an interaction or perhaps happen in ways that we hardly notice, recognizing which feeling we are experiencing is not always so simple. **Sometimes our attention is more focused on coping with the drama of a situation than the actual experience of our feelings.** Perhaps we have become a little too comfortable with the illusions fabricated by the unconscious avoidance or denial of our feelings.

Identifying our feelings by name ties us more directly to our inner emotional activity. **As our emotional sensations arise, using one of these 5 names for feelings – Mad, Sad, Glad, Afraid, and Ashamed – can create a vocabulary for making more specific connections between the physical sensations and the emotional content of the feeling we are experiencing in the moment.** John Bradshaw, a renowned pioneer of personal growth work, says that if we can name our feelings we can claim them and use them to heal ourselves.

Using more specific names for our feelings has other advantages. For instance, our language is teeming with elegant words to describe feelings. Although these words make intriguing literature and colorful conversation, this creative vocabulary can inadvertently distance us from our actual feelings. Using nonspecific names for our feelings can increase the ambiguity and minimization of our emotional experiences. Matching these less specific words to one of the specific 5 names can be helpful in connecting to a core feeling, especially if we are trying to expand our emotional range.

Take a moment to review The HEAL List of Feelings. Many of the words used to describe our emotions fall under one of the 5 specific names. The next time emotional energy stirs, touch the feeling by asking, *Am I feeling mad, sad, glad, afraid, or ashamed?*

We often experience more than one feeling at a time. This phenomenon seems contradictory and only adds confusion to our emotional state. Experiencing multiple feelings is not unusual and naming each acknowledges them separately and simultaneously.

Authentic feelings are not made; they just happen. They surface spontaneously as messengers from our needs and communicate information about our deeper state of satisfaction. Glad feelings of happiness and fulfillment reflect the loving and nurturing blessings and gifts we have received. Mad, sad, afraid, and ashamed feelings indicate that we have received less love and nurturance than we needed and may have unhealed wounds.

Most people know the difference between a glad feeling and a sad feeling. However, the differences between mad, sad, afraid, and shameful feelings are not as easy to distinguish. The following descriptions of feelings provide a basic guide to identify some different experiences and to interpret the messages our feelings are trying to relay about our needs.

Mad

Mad feelings can simmer like a smoldering fire, flaring occasionally and refusing to go out completely. At other times, our anger wants to strike out like a white-hot flash of lightning, scorching everything in close proximity.

Our mad feelings are associated with the blocking or separation of our needs from actual or anticipated sources of satisfaction. When our needs are frustrated abruptly and rudely, we tend to have a more intense emotional experience. In situations where our needs are less frustrated, the intensity of our feelings declines. The level of our angry emotional energy corresponds to the degree in which our need satisfaction is blocked.

Need Message: *My needs are important, and I want to get them met.*

Sad

One of the most difficult and unavoidable emotional sensations we experience as a human being is sadness. Each of us experiences feelings of sadness in our own unique way. Sad feelings can underwhelm or overwhelm our sense of contentment and well-being, appearing as a quiet, nagging uneasiness or an intense, inconsolable emptiness. Whether due to the loss of our most beloved relationship partner or the lack of physical comfort, feelings of sadness are usually caused by a change of connection with someone or something with which we were involved. The deeper and more intimate the relationship, the more intense and painful the loss is felt. Death, divorce, desertion, dislocation, disappearance, disappointment, disaster, and deceit are examples of loss and abrupt change of relationship that cause sad feelings to stir.

The significance of sadness is deeper than the mere absence or separation from a person or thing. Sad feelings are a cry of frustration from our need for love and our desire to be connected to others in satisfying, fulfilling ways. The greater the separation between the need and the source of its fulfillment, the more intense are the feelings of loss and sadness. In a way, sadness is a signal that we have lost or are about to lose our wholeness and harmony.

Need Message: *I have lost what I need, or I cannot get what I need.*

Glad

Glad feelings are the most pleasing and comfortable emotional sensations we experience, and the ones we spend most of our time pursuing. A happy sensation can be a friendly smile, the fullness and contentment that follows a good meal, or the warm and fuzzy sensation of a passionate kiss. Glad feelings can show up as giddiness and giggles or explosive outbursts of joyous laughter and song. If people are asked what they want most in life, a common response is, *I just want to be happy.*

We experience glad and happy feelings when our inner needs are fulfilled. The degree of satisfaction is enhanced by the extent we are aware and grateful that our needs are being met. Well-being and contentment are the product of having basic needs met. Joy and celebration occur when our higher needs, especially our need for love, are fulfilled.

Need Message: *I have what I need, and I am grateful.*

Afraid

The feeling of fear is one of the most pervasive, powerful emotions we experience. We can be so filled with fear that we become frozen in place, unable to move a muscle. Feeling afraid can disable us with shock, undermining our ability to make clear, independent choices. Fear can also jolt us into action, causing us to move more quickly than we ever could have imagined. Fearful feelings convey a sense of anxiety and dread that someone or something is about to frustrate, prevent, or interfere with our needs being met.

Need Message: *I am afraid my needs will not be satisfied.*

Shame

Shame can sting like a critic's arrow, numbing our entire body with contempt and loathing, or rise slowly within us like a silent red tide, drowning our confidence. The feelings of shame run the gamut between intense guilt about some transgression to perceptions of inadequacy, and may be veiled by arrogance, pride, or self-righteousness.

Shameful feelings sometimes result when we attempt to satisfy our needs at the expense of other people's needs. At other times our needs are frustrated because we do not feel adequate as human beings and, therefore, are undeserving of having our needs met.

Need Message: *I do not deserve to have my needs satisfied.*

Mad, sad, afraid, and ashamed feelings manifest themselves as sensations that are a combination of physical, mental, and spiritual suffering. All of these feelings can arise when our need satisfaction is frustrated, but each one brings a distinctly different message to our consciousness about our separation from or denial of the love we need.

Although seemingly triggered by external events, our feelings are actually spontaneously produced by our own internal state of neediness. Understanding how and why inner feelings happen unexpectedly also reveals the secret for honoring them. **Feelings are a call for love, and loving them honors them. It's all about love.**

An inevitable and undesirable consequence of treating our feelings like strangers is that they will eventually become just that, unwelcome, scary, odd, uncomfortable, unworthy of our attention, and something we seek to avoid. Honoring our feelings in loving ways by using their first names like the good, old friends they really are reconnects us to this vibrant part of Self. **Feelings are not only a unique part of our human and spiritual experience, but they are also essential for our learning, healing, growth, and general well-being.** The next time a feeling shows up, we will know how to extend a more cordial welcome.

141

The HEAL List of Feelings

Mad	Sad	Glad	Afraid	Shame
Angry	Apathetic	Calm	Alarmed	Ashamed
Annoyed	Blah	Comfortable	Anxious	Crazy
Bugged	Blue	Competent	Concerned	Dumb
Dangerous	Depressed	Content	Fear	Embarrassed
Displeased	Gloomy	Cool	Fearful	Foolish
Frustrated	Grief	Elated	Frightened	Hopeless
Harassed	Hurt	Free of Pain	Nervous	Humiliated
Hassled	In Pain	Fulfilled	Tense	Inadequate
Indignant	Low	Happy	Terrified	Incompetent
Irritated	Melancholy	Joyous	Threatened	Withdrawn
Mean	Mourning	Optimistic	Uneasy	Worthless
Resentful	Pessimistic	Playful	Uptight	
Spiteful	Rotten	Pleasure	Worried	
Vengeful	Sorrow	Relaxed		
	Unhappy	Relieved		
		Respected		
		Responsible		
		Safe		
		Satisfied		
		Secure		
		Valued		
		Well-being		

SEEKING
SELF

Follow the Arrows

When will you find a way,
And see yourself in every face?
You gotta go down inside yourself
And see and feel.
You gotta go down.
GARY ROSENBERG

The external world is busy with sensory information that can overload our ability to pay attention. With so many obvious human happenings on the outside, we can easily miss the subtle activities on the inside. Is our awareness so crowded with the obvious that we are missing something that may be happening just beneath the surface?

Explaining human relationship solely on what we see, hear, and touch may seem easier than delving deeper into Self through more intimate questioning and personal work. However, relying totally on observable information, like behaviors and actions, may be giving us a less than accurate picture of Self and might not fully reveal the underlying causes of what is happening to us. Feelings are the road signs that guide us toward the invisible answers that can only be found deeper within us.

Although blessed throughout our lives with many gifts, it is also our destiny to be wounded by many arrows.

DISCOVER
FEELINGS

These imaginary arrows represent real injuries resulting from less than loving and nurturing relationship choices that we make or endure from others. Following these symbols of our wounds leads us to the source of our feelings and neediness.

Imagine a human form consisting of three layers that illustrate our behaviors (the visible Self), our feelings (the partially hidden Self), and our needs (the core Self). The behavior layer shows words, actions, and deeds that are externally observed. The feeling layer is comprised of two parts: one that can be seen on the surface, such as facial expressions and body language, and another that is located just beneath the surface, a hidden pool of emotional energy. At the center lies the needy core, where our yearning for attention and satisfaction sparks the energy of our feelings and ultimately drives our behaviors.

Now visualize a large arrow protruding from this imaginary human body, violating its delicate anatomy and piercing each layer as it points down the path to our inner core. Each arrow, symbolic of pain and lost wholeness, represents an individual wound and remains embedded until healed. The feathered tail of this arrow represents a range of behaviors, from unpleasant to aggressive, that indicates trouble to the sensitive observer.

To discover more about the source of our suffering, we move further down the arrow's shaft to the surface of the body. Here, we notice the external expression of our feelings, such as red faces, angry grimaces, crying, contorted or slumped posture, and blank stares. These can be evidence of old or new wounds that occur when feelings are suppressed, inhibited, or medicated.

Further down, the other part of each feeling fills our body with a variety of sensations. Encountering immediate emotional turbulence may indicate we are dealing with a fresh wound that is still sensitive, while confused or mixed-up sensations may mean that the wound is old and unhealed. At this point on the journey, if we are numb or void of feelings, it may signal a very old, unhealed wound whose pain is deeply repressed. Feelings are always present, flowing, active, and inviting our attention.

Finally, we arrive at the end of the arrow's shaft, where the source of our pain is located. Symbolized by the arrowhead, our frustrated needs can be found at the heart of our woundedness. When the natural process for getting our needs met is frustrated, we find ourselves experiencing a spectrum of emotional states, ranging from mild discomfort to extreme distress. Like the shaft connecting feathers to the arrowhead, feelings intricately connect external behaviors to unfulfilled needs. Feelings of mad, sad, afraid, and shame are the body's way of communicating the pain of woundedness and calling out for the healing love and attention needed.

Too often, we judge Self as bad, flawed, or inadequate. **If we look only at the surface or the quality of the behavior, it is easy to assign blame and shame to some destructive choice or action.** We might not be so quick to judge and condemn behavior, once we discover the underlying damage and hurt that exists within each of us. Seeing Self as a wounded being creates a deeper understanding that evokes compassion and forgiveness. Following the arrows of our wounds leads us to many of the answers we seek about Self.

Way 4

Nurture Needs

Nearly every one of us is starving to be appreciated, to be the recipient of that most supreme compliment — that we are loved. . . . Loving means standing on our own two feet, counting on ourselves, making our own way. We may, at times, need the help of others, but we cannot expect them to satisfy needs which are solely ours to satisfy.

Leo Buscaglia

Following My Arrows

Reared to be a perfect Southern gentleman, I was never encouraged to experience my feelings or to understand my needs. Family tradition and culture urged me to control and suppress my needs, especially my emotional and spiritual ones. These learned habits were partly to blame for the hurtful behaviors and attitudes that I adopted in my life. Changing old habits has proven to be hard, despite the suffering they have caused.

Growing up in a home of material privilege, I was blessed with physical comfort and a loving childhood. Despite the many benefits offered by this lifestyle, our family relationships were not always nurturing and positive, resulting in many disagreements, conflicts, and woundings.

One of my earliest woundings happened when my parents decided to send me to military school at the tender age of eleven. Although the intention was to provide me with a better educational opportunity, this forced separation from my family and childhood friends was abrupt and painful. For the first time, I knew the ache of loneliness, and my sense of abandonment and unworthiness felt like a huge empty hole in my gut. Instead of being filled with love that I so desperately needed, I was filled with anguish, disbelief, shame, and sadness.

At military school, fear was my frequent companion, as I cautiously navigated the halls and playgrounds that were dominated by older, bigger, and sometimes dangerous boys. We were all just trying to survive, but the law of the jungle called on the strong to prey on the weak and less experienced. If these troublemaking peers did not get me, there were paddle-toting commandants on guard, anxious to enforce the rules if I stepped out of line. Crybabies did not last long in such a place, so I quickly learned to fight when trapped and to hide, deny, and suppress my real feelings, especially my tears.

My life's training and environment were teaching me that I could get some of the love I needed if I did what I was supposed to do. The unpleasant difficulties and drama that occurred over time were a reflection of the wounds I received at home and at military school. They continued to fester beneath the surface, forming an unsure foundation for my adolescence and adulthood.

I actually rebelled against conforming to my family's view of who I should be. Unaware of what my feelings were trying to tell me, I pursued and accomplished many goals in my personal and business life that *should* have made me happy. Unfortunately, no level of success satisfied my needs, nor would it, until I understood what was really going on deeper within my Self.

Despite an external appearance of success, the joy in my life was overshadowed by emptiness and dissatisfaction, and my attempts to nurture my needs with material things failed. I began to explore a wide range of methods for medicating my feelings, but these choices only frustrated my needs and impeded my emotional and spiritual growth. When medicating and its false satisfactions no longer eased my pain, I was finally willing to look deeper for the causes of my suffering. I had always wanted to understand the problems in my relationships and find what was missing.

Hitting bottom, surrendering, and embracing recovery saved me from the perils of my addictions and helped me to see the connection between my feelings and needs. Following my arrows led me to my greatest wound, a lack of love caused by my experiences of rejection, abandonment, and inadequacy. Once I began to understand how all these disjointed pieces of my life were connected, I was slowly able to lovingly tend my brokenness. At first my progress was almost imperceptible. But with tremendous patience, honesty, and loving support, I was able to move slowly toward the wholeness of acceptance, commitment, and adequacy.

Standing on the firm footing of my men's group, 12-Step programs, and personal growth work, I continue to deal with the hassles, conflicts, and drama of my life in a good way. I can actually have my feelings, even though allowing my grief remains difficult, and my joy is still shadowed by an old, inner monologue that haunts me with presumed unworthiness. There are still moments when life presses down hard, but the extreme stress and destructive behaviors of the past are gone. Today, I can accept progress over perfection; I build rather than destroy; and I am learning to heal, not just continue to hurt. Thanks to following my own arrows, I am more alive, well, and real than ever.

Nurture Needs

*In my youth I used alcohol and cocaine in order to cover up
the pain that I felt...like the pain of the emptiness inside
that you don't know how to fill.*
MELANIE GRIFFITH

Discovering and honoring feelings can lead us
directly to the source of pain and joy in our
relationships, our needs. Although our needs offer crucial
guidance in the search for understanding Self, their function
is often hidden, missed, or misunderstood. Needs are to
Self as Self is to relationships. Without an understanding of the foundational roles that needs and Self play in
our interactions, we cannot understand why we behave
the way we do. Our understanding of needs and their
significance has been impacted by social, cultural, and
technical evolution. These misperceptions about needs
have strongly influenced our view of Self and the ways we
choose to frustrate or nurture our needs.

One cost of this evolutionary progress is the
dehumanization of Self. Unknowingly, we may be setting ourselves up for failure and disappointment while
simultaneously becoming experts at frustrating our own
needs. Unrealistic expectations of Self or others, external
influences of family and culture, and reliance on material

possessions and comforts can undermine our ability to take care of Self.

As we expand awareness of our needs and learn to honor our feelings, it may be useful to imagine the emptiness inside us that longs for attention as a need bowl. This symbolic bowl functions like an empty belly that hungers for food. Our need bowl yearns to be filled with something. That something is the amazing, nurturing energy of love.

How we choose to fill our need bowl can mean the difference between a life of anger, sadness, fear, and shame or one filled with joy and abundance. Our need bowl, the Holy Grail in the search for Self, connects us directly to the essential core of Self, that part of us that desires to love and be loved.

View Needs as Natural

You can't always get what you want,
but if you try sometimes,
you just might find,
you get what you need!
THE ROLLING STONES

From one-celled organisms to more complex life forms, all living creatures have essential needs that require fulfillment in order for them to survive and exist in harmony. Each has physiological processes that make it possible for them to determine their needs and to fill them. Denying this divine design is unnatural and unhealthy.

Human beings were created with both basic and higher needs. In the past, satisfying even the most basic needs was difficult. In modern times it is our higher needs that many of us find more challenging to identify and satisfy. If we are fortunate enough to have our basic needs met, we can focus more of our attention on fulfilling our higher needs, which profoundly influences the quality of our life and relationships.

Higher needs stimulate feelings and motivate behaviors in ways that are directly connected to their level of satisfaction. When our need bowl is full, we feel joyful and content because all our needs have been temporarily filled. If our need bowl is less than full and needs go unmet, we may feel angry, sad, afraid, or ashamed. The inner prompting of our physiological processes heightens our sensitivity to our need bowl and to its desire to be filled.

Maslow's Hierarchy of Needs

Intensive studies of human needs have led to many theories on human motivation and behavior. One such theory proposed by psychologist Abraham H. Maslow declared that people have the capacity to achieve well-being by making rational decisions that enable them to satisfy their needs. Based on his theory, Maslow developed a well-known hierarchy of needs that prioritized them and the logic associated with their satisfaction. He was one of the first to distinguish between basic human needs, such as shelter, water, food, sex, and security, and higher human needs, such as love, acceptance, belonging, and esteem.

Maslow's work demonstrated how needs motivate behavior. He claimed that basic, physiological needs must be met before we would aspire to fill higher ones. As the desire to meet higher needs increases, the stage is set to move up the need pyramid. According to his thinking, we all ultimately seek to realize our human potential by fulfilling our needs.

Our needs define who we are. When we interfere with our natural and necessary functions, we risk corrupting our very design. Satisfying our needs creates wholeness and health. We live in an exciting part of the history of the Greater Human Family because there are so many opportunities to explore, understand, and satisfy needs, especially our higher human need for love.

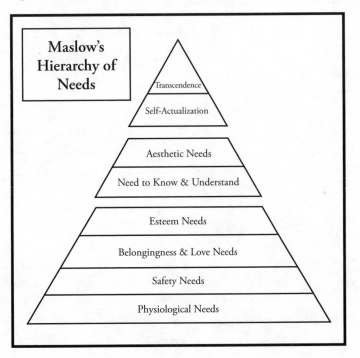

Maslow's Hierarchy of Needs

Transcendence
Self-Actualization
Aesthetic Needs
Need to Know & Understand
Esteem Needs
Belongingness & Love Needs
Safety Needs
Physiological Needs

NURTURE
NEEDS

Understand the Role of Needs

*When we allow ourselves to experience our emotions and
accept them, sometimes this allows us to move
to a deeper level of awareness where important
information presents itself.*
NATHANIEL BRANDEN

Although needs are both natural and necessary,
their functions are not clearly explained to us as
we grow from infancy to adulthood. One reason for this
lack of clarity occurs because needs, like feelings, are not
always easy to perceive or understand. For instance, our
higher needs for love and validation are not as easy to
detect as our basic needs for food or water. Responding
to an empty stomach's growl is effortless, if food is available.
On the other hand, it can be much more difficult to
recognize feelings as the rumblings of our higher need
bowl. Perhaps this is why we are not any more skilled at
filling them with the love they require, even when love
is present. **Learning to name our needs, like learning to
name our feelings, can be very useful for increasing our
understanding of their related roles and for strengthening
connections to both.**

**Many people have been conditioned to believe that
there is something wrong in meeting their own natural**

human needs, so they project their guilt or shame about their needs on others. There may be some basis for postponing, delaying, or managing needs at particular times, like rationing food consumption during famine or exercising restraint from sexual activity just because we are in the mood. Even though essential to living and relating, some people would deny the importance of need satisfaction to health and wholeness. Needs, one of the miracles of our humanness, deserve our blessings, not our curses.

Another source of confusion around needs and their role is the difficulty of distinguishing needs from wants. For clarity, let us agree to the following difference in meaning for these words. **Needs make a difference to our health and wholeness, while wants represent our desires for nonessential things or qualities.**

Another useful distinction between wants and needs is that we survive the disappointment of an unsatisfied want, while failure to fulfill a need can lead to mad, sad, afraid, or ashamed feelings that accompany a genuine deprivation of love. Unmet needs can cause suffering, while giving up a want or whim carries fewer negative consequences and may actually nurture our well-being. **Our wants are optional; our needs are not.**

Understanding need satisfaction can provide the information for the nurturing we need to create personal health. Because our needs are rarely satisfied completely, they continue to call and motivate us to heal and grow. We behave and feel the way we do because of what we need. Understanding the role of needs reveals the mysteries of Self.

NURTURE
NEEDS

Imagine Filling Self with Love

What happens in your innermost being
is worthy of your whole love.
RAINER MARIE RILKE

The significance of human needs may seem obvious to many people, but the long legacy of emotional and spiritual suffering indicates we still do not know how to satisfy our needs effectively. Dysfunctional and destructive relationship behaviors continue to be an integral part of our shared human history, following us like some dark, collective shadow. The search for Self can challenge this heritage by shining light on higher needs and showing us what it takes to satisfy them.

Imagine our higher needs as a bottomless need bowl that we carry everywhere we go. Like the wandering Buddhist priests and their begging bowls, we hold out our need bowl with the humble and hopeful expectation it will be filled. The function of this symbolic bowl is to hold something essential for health and well-being that is continually consumed. The bottomless nature demands that it be replenished from various internal and external sources again and again.

Our higher needs signal that there is an emptiness within us that requires filling. What is this powerful, fulfilling element for which our needs so desperately long? It is love. **Love is the energy of our spiritual being and ultimately fills our higher need bowls.**

We look for sources of love to fill our need bowls. Some sources flow readily from within, while other sources emerge only after repeated demands for attention. **When our need bowl is full of love, we experience glad feelings and contentment. When it has less love, our neediness becomes apparent as sad feelings and anxiety characterize our behavior.**

External Sources of Love

Consider these three external sources of loving energy that exist in our world and contribute to our need bowl: our higher power, other people, and material things.

Higher Power

For many of us, a higher power is a spiritual source of love, such as the God of our understanding, angels, or even forces of nature. We each create a relationship with this higher power that serves to fill our need bowl from a divine source of love. We rely on a higher power to provide unconditional love and to help us understand the meaning of life and death.

Other People

During the early years of life, we depend on our family or nurturing group to meet our need for love. Later, we discover additional sources of support that include partners, friends, children, co-workers, and members of our social, religious, and cultural communities. We extend our need bowl to these people for contributions that satisfy our needs for attention, affection, respect, acknowledgment, and belonging.

Material Things

Food, water, clothing, and shelter are a few of the material things that fill our basic needs. In an attempt to satisfy our higher needs, it is easy to fall under the seductive allure of material comforts. Physical objects and places, like expensive vehicles, big houses in exclusive neighborhoods, designer clothing, extravagant vacations, high-paying jobs, and societal memberships, are examples of things that do provide significant, yet intangible, benefits. For example, a good job provides income for purchasing material goods, but more significant is the nurturing that comes from a job's ability to endow a sense of meaning, pride, and Self-sufficiency. A vehicle, even an inexpensive one, is another example of a material item that is more than just a means of transportation. It nurtures the owner by providing mobility and a sense of independence.

Although some material things do offer limited intrinsic value, placing too much emphasis on substituting material items and money for love is likely to result in need frustration. This approach to fulfillment is not uncommon in the materialistic culture of today.

No matter how hard we try or how much external loving energy we garner, the nature of our need bowl is such that it cannot be adequately filled from an external source alone. **Our need bowl requires a mixture of loving energy from various sources, including a source from inside us.**

Internal Source of Love

Our wholeness greatly depends upon our ability to supplement our need bowl internally, rather than relying solely upon external contributions. Each of us has an internal source of love. The origin and nature of this reservoir is not completely understood, but it is essential because this is the Self-love that can be used to fill our need bowl.

As our search approaches the very center of Self, we discover that the need bowl is actually a human heart. **Each heart feels the inner emptiness that yearns to be filled with love and desires to reach out in loving ways to others.** This natural, innate capacity to love, heal, and grow is the spiritual common ground on which we build our relationship with Self and others.

Match Feelings to Needs

The more directly we can connect our feelings to our needs,
the easier it is to respond compassionately to our needs.
MARSHALL B. ROSENBERG

Every feeling that we experience matches directly
to a need that calls for satisfaction. Our feelings
percolate slowly or rush rapidly to the surface whenever
the level of loving energy in our need bowl fluctuates.
By paying attention to these feelings, their meaning can
be uncovered and matched to their underlying needs.
**Matching feelings to needs is a skill that turns awareness
into information and improves with practice.**

When mad, sad, afraid, and ashamed feelings happen,
they are signaling us that we have frustrated needs.
In contrast, when we have glad feelings, our needs are
enjoying an abundance of loving and nurturing energy.
Marshall Rosenberg, a psychologist who has done
extensive work in the area of nonviolent communications,
has developed a useful list of feelings that he matches with
unfulfilled and fulfilled needs.

NURTURE
NEEDS

Feelings When Needs Are Not Fulfilled

Angry	Frightened	Nervous
Annoyed	Frustrated	Overwhelmed
Concerned	Helpless	Puzzled
Confused	Hopeless	Reluctant
Disappointed	Impatient	Sad
Discouraged	Irritated	Uncomfortable
Distressed	Lonely	

Feelings When Needs Are Fulfilled

Amazed	Hopeful	Relieved
Comfortable	Inspired	Stimulated
Confident	Intrigued	Surprised
Eager	Joyous	Thankful
Energetic	Moved	Touched
Fulfilled	Optimistic	Trustful
Glad	Proud	

While emotional messages may help other people understand what we feel and need, the most important recipient of this information is our own consciousness. Listening to, acknowledging, and then matching our feelings to their corresponding needs help achieve more effective need satisfaction and the joy and happiness that accompanies such fulfillment. We match feelings to needs by observing any emotional energy that comes up relative to an event or thought and asking ourselves the following questions.

Match Feelings to Needs

> *What is the name of this feeling?*
> *What underlying need matches this feeling?*
> *What is the name of my need?*
> *How can I satisfy it?*

It sounds so simple. Yet, understanding our relationships in terms of behaviors, feelings, and needs rather than just behaviors widens our view considerably. Feelings are the visible envoys of our needs, those bowls that cannot be seen, only perceived. **Matching our feelings to our needs empowers us to interpret their messages so that we can make choices to directly nurture our needs.**

The following expanded lists of feelings have been contributed by Jean Handley of Turning Point Partners, a non-profit organization dedicated to creating authentic, peaceful community. These lists further highlight the connection between feelings and needs.

How We Feel When Our Needs Are *Not* Being Met

Afraid	Confused	Edgy
Aggravated	Cool	Embarrassed
Agitated	Cross	Embittered
Alarmed	Dejected	Exasperated
Aloof	Depressed	Exhausted
Angry	Despairing	Fatigued
Anguished	Despondent	Fearful
Annoyed	Detached	Fidgety
Anxious	Disaffected	Forlorn
Apathetic	Disappointed	Frightened
Apprehensive	Discouraged	Frustrated
Aroused	Disenchanted	Furious
Ashamed	Disgruntled	Gloomy
Beat	Disgusted	Guilty
Bewildered	Disheartened	Harried
Bitter	Dismayed	Heavy
Blah	Displeased	Helpless
Blue	Disquieted	Hesitant
Bored	Distressed	Horrible
Brokenhearted	Disturbed	Horrified
Chagrined	Downcast	Hostile
Cold	Downhearted	Hot
Concerned	Dull	Humdrum

How We Feel When Our Needs Are *Not* Being Met,
continued

Hurt
Impatient
Indifferent
Intense
Irate
Irked
Irritated
Jealous
Jittery
Keyed-up
Lazy
Leery
Lethargic
Listless
Lonely
Mad
Mean
Miserable
Mopey
Morose
Mournful
Nervous
Nettled

Numb
Overwhelmed
Panicky
Passive
Perplexed
Pessimistic
Puzzled
Rancorous
Reluctant
Repelled
Resentful
Restless
Sad
Scared
Sensitive
Shaky
Shocked
Skeptical
Sleepy
Sorrowful
Sorry
Spiritless
Startled

Surprised
Suspicious
Tepid
Terrified
Tired
Troubled
Uncomfortable
Unconcerned
Uneasy
Unglued
Unnerved
Unsteady
Upset
Uptight
Vexed
Weary
Wistful
Withdrawn
Woeful
Worried
Wretched

NURTURE
NEEDS

How We Feel When Our Needs Are Being Met

Absorbed	*Contented*	*Free*
Adventurous	*Cool*	*Friendly*
Affectionate	*Curious*	*Fulfilled*
Alert	*Dazzled*	*Glad*
Alive	*Delighted*	*Gleeful*
Amazed	*Eager*	*Glorious*
Animated	*Ebullient*	*Glowing*
Appreciative	*Ecstatic*	*Good-humored*
Ardent	*Effervescent*	*Grateful*
Aroused	*Elated*	*Gratified*
Astonished	*Enchanted*	*Happy*
Blissful	*Encouraged*	*Helpful*
Breathless	*Energetic*	*Hopeful*
Buoyant	*Engrossed*	*Inquisitive*
Calm	*Enlivened*	*Inspired*
Carefree	*Enthusiastic*	*Intense*
Cheerful	*Excited*	*Interested*
Comfortable	*Exhilarated*	*Intrigued*
Complacent	*Expansive*	*Invigorated*
Composed	*Expectant*	*Involved*
Concerned	*Exultant*	*Joyous, joyful*
Confident	*Fascinated*	*Jubilant*

How We Feel When Our Needs Are Being Met
continued

Keyed-up	*Proud*	*Stimulated*
Loving	*Quiet*	*Surprised*
Mellow	*Radiant*	*Tender*
Merry	*Rapturous*	*Thankful*
Mirthful	*Refreshed*	*Thrilled*
Moved	*Relaxed*	*Touched*
Optimistic	*Relieved*	*Tranquil*
Overjoyed	*Satisfied*	*Trusting*
Overwhelmed	*Secured*	*Upbeat*
Peaceful	*Sensitive*	*Warm*
Perky	*Serene*	*Wide-awake*
Pleasant	*Spellbound*	*Wonderful*
Pleased	*Splendid*	*Zestful*

NURTURE
NEEDS

Accept Progress over Perfection

I was taught that the way of progress
is neither swift nor easy.
MARIE CURIE

L ife consists of many cyclic processes that tend to begin, build, and ultimately reach a level of completion, only to recede and repeat the cycle again. So it is with our needs. Our need bowl is bottomless by nature, so accepting this reality relieves us from the unrealistic expectations that all our needs can be met. Need satisfaction is not guaranteed. The expectation for perfect satisfaction of our needs is unattainable and unrealistic and only sets us up for frustration and disappointment. We can never be completely safe, full, seen, valued, or happy.

Sometimes external need satisfaction can more easily be achieved by letting go of any expected outcome. Trying too hard to gain fulfillment can result in barriers that hinder satisfaction. For example, in making new friends, we might attempt to do so by being overly friendly, talking loudly, or standing too closely to people. These efforts may prove counterproductive, and the very attention we seek may be withheld or directed toward others. The need to be noticed may be more easily satisfied by letting go of our fear of not getting attention and waiting patiently for recognition and inclusion.

Some people base their sense of Self-worth on their hopes for attaining fame, fortune, and the admiration of others. Ironically, fame, wealth, and title are no guarantee. People who can surrender their obsession to be extraordinary often find more happiness when they are willing to accept and appreciate the abundance that already exists in their ordinary lives. Accepting progress over the urge to reach perfection teaches us that we do not have to be famous in order to be loved, valued, respected, and desired.

Awareness of the insatiable nature of needs allows us to surrender the unrealistic goal of complete satisfaction. When we learn to let go of perfection, real progress can be made towards enjoying satisfying lives and relationships.

Relate to Real Self

There is no need to run outside for better seeing. Nor to peer from a window. Rather reside in the center of your being. The more you leave it, the less you learn.

LAO-TZE

Many of us relate to an inner Self that resembles the disjointed, chaotic, cubistic image of a Picasso portrait. This perception of who we are seems to be a discombobulated patchwork, painted by the relentless chatter of external voices, past and present, admonishing us to be the person we *should be*, *have to be*, or *ought to be*. **Each of us has a *should be* Self that is a product of the demands and opinions of others and which encumbers any attempt to discover and relate to who we really are. The person they need us to be is not necessarily the person we need to be.**

This identity crisis is actually a conflict between our needs and the needs of others. Satisfying our actual needs means relating to real Self and cultivating an authentic friendship of love and acceptance. We will never experience genuine satisfaction if we are trying to meet the needs of a *should be* Self.

Listening to real Self acknowledges our feelings, needs, and inner voice. Often this quiet voice is difficult to hear over the loud and overpowering debates conducted in our heads between numerous *should be* Selves. Slowing down, being in the present moment, and meditating are all practices that help us attune to our own inner voice.

Real Self celebrates our known talents and abilities while also embracing the side we do not know as well, where the wounds of unmet higher needs reside. **This shadow side of Self is the part we hide, deny, and repress from the outside world and from our own awareness. Shadow is that place from which our painful feelings, frustrated needs, and destructive behaviors emanate.** Bringing light gently into this shadow safely uncovers family secrets, relationship fears, and emotional pain so that healing can begin. By sending loving energy directly to our natural needs, we shrink our shadow side and create a more whole, healthy Self.

Relating to real Self is not selfish. Many societies actually encourage people to focus their attention on the needs of the group rather than the individual. Even societies that value the individual characterize excessive interest in the Self as selfish behavior. Too much internal attention can become potentially destructive behavior that negatively affects other relationships; however, emphasizing the needs of others at the expense of honoring our own also risks harmful consequences. Relating to real Self may actually decrease selfish behavior and encourage positive regard of others.

Seeking Self is a journey that takes us down an inner path to our own answers and wisdom. Accepting all parts of Self, no matter how wounded or scarred, directly nurtures our needs, healing and strengthening us in magnificent ways.

179

NURTURE
NEEDS

Realize Our Significance

*If only you could sense how important you are to the lives
of those you meet, how important you can be to
people you may never even dream of.*
FRED "MISTER" ROGERS

Our lives are filled with a relentless flow of subliminal messages that suggest we should improve ourselves or we risk leading a less meaningful existence. These messages can instill us with self-doubt and erode our perception of self-worth and adequacy. **When our higher needs to be loved, accepted, and valued go unfulfilled, we can be driven to seek satisfaction in obsessive or unhealthy ways.**

While external influences may appear to be harmless, they eventually take their toll on our wholeness and well being, and we begin to believe the demeaning messages from family, friends, and the media. Somewhere along the way, it is possible to lose sight of our own value and become stuck in the perception that we are not good enough. Only through the realization that we each possess unique talents, abilities, and gifts are we able to reclaim our significance.

We can interpret other people's words and actions in ways that undermine our level of confidence and personal contentment, perpetuating this shadow of inadequacy. Media messages also corrupt our view of Self through the constant promotion of products and services that promise to improve our image, appearance, comfort, or satisfaction. Many of us turn our perception of powerlessness into one of inadequacy, especially if we have not yet accepted that we are powerless over certain things. The desire for instantaneous wealth, physical beauty, and success can be a powerful motivator that compels us to reach for significance in ways that are measured externally by rank, money, possessions, power, awards, or fame.

Apprehensions about our significance can be unintentionally created in ways that are not always the result of judgment or criticism. They can be triggered by simple actions, such as special attention given to a sibling, relative, or another person while we are ignored. The key feature in this dynamic is not so much what others receive as what we do not. **If our need to be seen, heard, or valued is not nurtured, we often perceive Self as inadequate or in competition with others. This negative energy is incorporated into our entire being, as we confuse inaccurate messages with reality.**

When the conditions of our worthiness are based on the remarkable accomplishments of our ancestors or the legacy of cultural heroes, we often establish unrealistically high expectations that set us up for failure or that deepen our perceptions of insignificance. We can be inspired and motivated by the greatness of others and attempting to emulate their efforts is an honorable intention. However, the choice to use some ideal as the yardstick by which we measure Self may actually distract us from our real purpose and responsibility in the present. Our significance can be realized by developing our own talents and abilities, instead of trying to be something or someone we are not.

Our tendency to assume responsibility for things we cannot control reinforces feelings of inadequacy. Focusing attention and expending energy on changing that which we can change empower us to make effective contributions. Saving the world is not our responsibility; it is enough to merely serve it. We can realize our significance through personal, meaningful action, such as giving support when someone asks for help or by making a contribution to a specific cause.

The inner perception of insignificance does more harm than any criticism. Each of us has wonderful gifts to share with family, friends, and communities, and any inaccurate perceptions of Self to the contrary likely are initiated and reinforced by external influences. Personal attitudes, beliefs, and goals are ours to choose and help us become happy, compassionate, and generous individuals. **We realize the significance of Self when we choose to contribute to every encounter and interaction in loving and nurturing ways.**

NURTURE
NEEDS

Notice Ways We Frustrate Needs

Your Vision will become clear only
when you look into your heart...
Who looks outside, dreams.
Who looks inside, awakens.

CARL JUNG

An unseen or unmet need is a frustrated need. Virtually invisible to the human eye and more subtle than our feelings and behaviors, our needs can be easily frustrated. Each call of our needs is an opportunity to identify, understand, and nurture them as fully as possible in that very moment. Missing an opportunity to do so may cause a wound, a state of being less than, which requires healing for restoring the Self to wholeness.

Looking at the following ways we frustrate our own needs provides valuable insight into how to achieve more need satisfaction.

Lack of Awareness of Needs

Needs usually get our attention indirectly through the stimulation of feelings and the motivation of behaviors. Lack of awareness of our needs makes it difficult if not impossible to nurture them and can be very harmful to our mental, physical, emotional, and spiritual health. We can't nurture what we don't notice.

Ignoring Needs

Even when our needs generate feelings of pain or discomfort, we often choose not to acknowledge them in the moment. Viewing our needs as irrelevant or selfish makes it easier to dismiss them, but doing so can cause deep wounds and deprive us of an opportunity to heal. **We carry these ignored needs into our relationships, hoping they will eventually be noticed and healed. The silent pain of these ignored needs is evident in the feelings and behaviors we display in our encounters.** Ignored needs do not go away.

Postponing Needs

Often we recognize that our bodies, minds, or spirits are in need of something, but we postpone gratification. Although there may be situations where delayed gratification is appropriate, postponing need satisfaction potentially jeopardizes opportunities for fulfillment. We may get more than once chance to fill a need, and yet each opportunity is unique and may never come again in quite the same way.

Judging Needs

Many people want to judge needs as good or bad. Whether we evaluate them as worthy or unworthy of attention, to judge needs keeps us from accepting a natural and necessary part of Self. **Going into our heads** rather than our hearts separates us from our needs and reduces the chances for need satisfaction.

Judged needs cause dysfunctional pain, like unhealthy cravings, compulsions, or obsessions. Even so, some of us find it more alluring to control our needs than to satisfy them. Judging our needs away can become routine, rather than determining what they mean and how they can be satisfied in healthy ways. Judgment impairs our ability to give our needs the loving care they deserve.

Condemning Needs

Allowing the opinions of others to influence our choices can twist judgment into actual condemnation of a need. We do not live in total isolation; therefore, meeting our individual needs means considering them in the larger context of the community's needs. Both the individual and the group share responsibility for mutual need satisfaction.

Fear-based thinking compels people to attempt to manage the world by condemning certain needs in order to attain a false sense of security. This behavior interferes with our ability to understand and satisfy specific individual needs, leaving us hurt and empty. Condemning needs can become a habit that negatively affects our ability to create meaningful connection with Self. Our needs do not seek our approval; they simply seek recognition and care.

Blaming and Shaming Needs

Blaming and shaming are abusive behaviors whose energies can be accepted into our core being. This energy can be unconsciously converted into negative messages that eventually become our beliefs and promote an unhealthy perception of Self. When our lives are lived on the receiving end of blaming and shaming behaviors, our perceived inadequacy can undermine our relationship with Self. Blaming and shaming send the message that we don't deserve to have our needs met.

Giving Away Our Personal Power

We can hope, ask, or expect others to fill our need bowl, but in this process we unwittingly choose to give away our personal power to take care of Self. **Other people have a limited capacity to provide us with the meaningful satisfaction we seek, and we have no real power over their willingness or ability to nurture us.**

Another way we give power away is by blaming other people for our frustrated needs. Blaming does nothing to achieve real need satisfaction and diverts us from paying attention to the inner calling of our needs. Taking care of these is primarily the responsibility of Self.

Remembering that it is our responsibility to take care of our own needs helps promote balance, happiness, and inner harmony. Relinquishing our power to others limits our ability to satisfy needs and sets us up for disappointment and the mad, sad, and fearful feelings that accompany frustrated needs.

Inhibiting Our Feelings

Feelings are messengers telling us what our needs require. Inhibiting feelings suppresses these messages and creates a false sense of satisfaction by producing an illusion of fulfillment and artificial feelings of contentment. When we stifle the messages from our needs, we can't nurture them. The choice to inhibit feelings suppresses the very information that would reduce our suffering.

Inability to Match Behaviors to Feelings and Feelings to Needs

The more we learn about Self, the more we realize and appreciate our own complexity. **We have many needs and, depending on the relative state of fullness, each need sends out a spectrum of feeling energy, ranging from mad to glad.** The number of behaviors that accompany this emotional energy is staggering, which makes matching them even more difficult. Frustrated needs happen when we cannot match them to their corresponding feelings and behaviors.

In trying to meet our needs, we may make some choices that actually prevent their satisfaction. Frustrated needs are often caused by a lack of skills and understanding of what is needed to successfully satisfy them. Self is often the target of loving intentions that have a detrimental impact. What is offered lovingly as constructive criticism, unsolicited advice, or ideas that are for our own good can have the opposite effect. These are some of the ways Self learns to blame, shame, judge, and even condemn its own design. Again, our relationship environment and lack of awareness set us up to deny our own nature by ignoring and postponing what really is good for us.

Seeking
Self

Learn to Nurture Needs

If we truly pay attention, our essence takes over and directs
our attention and responses in…a resourceful way.
MICHAEL RAY AND ROCHELLE MYERS

Now we can see how finely honed skills can be used to frustrate our needs in the name of love. The reward for this acquired expertise becomes a restless, underlying sense of neediness that many of us experience. Even though we don't intentionally choose to suffer through feelings of inadequacy, anger, sadness, fear, and shame, we do suffer. Perhaps we are merely blind to the consequences of these choices and to the compelling thirst for nurture caused by frustrated needs.

Humankind may have achieved unparalleled heights of intellectual and technological development, but we are still mere neophytes at giving and receiving the love we need. The next crucial step on our path to seeking Self is learning to nurture our own needs. Here are some ways we can tap into our internal reservoirs to fill our own need bowl with the love that can nurture Self into a state of wholeness and health. The following choices help us begin the shift from frustrating our needs to nurturing them.

Become More Sensitive

Being sensitive and attuned to the messages embedded in our feelings and behaviors give us helpful information to fill our needs so that we do not then ignore, deny, and postpone them. The more aware we are of these telltale signs, the more likely we are to nurture needs in the present moment.

Sensitivity connects us directly to our neediness.

Be Grateful

Gratitude is an extension of a positive attitude. One of the most empowering choices we have for nurturing our needs and implementing change in our life is our attitude. Choosing to view needs as a positive part of life gives us a clearer understanding of who we are and what we need to experience the joy of satisfaction.

No matter how much nurturing we receive, there never seems to be enough valuing, listening, or loving to fill our need bowl completely. Just as we relax in the joy and peace of having enough, the nurturing we have received is already draining away.

Perception creates our reality. If we view our bowl as half-empty, we are choosing an attitude that invites scarcity. Perceiving our bowl as half-full reflects an attitude of gratitude that manifests fullness and satisfaction. The blessings we desire and deserve are only temporary and our thankfulness for them is a choice we can make that fosters a perception of fulfillment.

Gratitude for what we have, while we have it, is nurturing.

Discern and Celebrate Needs

Need satisfaction is a two-part process that involves seeing a need and then meeting it. Somewhere between the seeing and the meeting, we make decisions based on the information we perceive about a need and how to meet it. Judgment is a common choice that, when made out of fear, characterizes a need as right or wrong, thereby negating its value and blocking the satisfaction process before it even gets started. Discernment, a more love-based option, is a way of determining the importance of a particular need. In this process we see each need as valid and seek completion by focusing on the requirements and impact of need satisfaction.

All needs want to be celebrated, not just tolerated or medicated. Needs are natural. When we accept and care for them for what they are, we validate our natural yearning for love, attention, direction, affection, respect, kindness, support, and understanding. **Discernment and celebration empower us to make thoughtful choices that maintain a healthy balance between need satisfaction and the negative consequences.**

Our job is to fill our need bowl lovingly and gently, not to judge it.

Practice Acceptance and Forgiveness

Reversing the frustrating effects of judging, blaming, and shaming messages begins with acceptance and forgiveness. Acceptance happens by acknowledging that we really are good enough just as we are. Then we can let go of old, negative messages, forgive our Self for believing them, and forgive others for delivering them. We are perfect, even in our imperfection. **Our pains and wounds are actually gifts and lessons that provide opportunity to heal and nurture.**

Acceptance and forgiveness are acts of Self-love.

Use the Power of Affirmations

Unfulfilled needs leave us with personal wounds that haunt us and undermine our esteem, adequacy, and peace of mind. Affirmations are positive messages that reinforce our sense of worth. Their healing power reprograms the dialogues playing over and over in our head, breaking the unhealthy cycle of blame and shame. Daily affirmations turn negative beliefs into positive possibilities.

Affirmations align Self with love and powerfully summon what we desire in life by declaring positive intentions.

Recover Lost Power

We lose our personal power when we rely on others to nurture our needs. **Whether we give away our power or it is taken away, recovering lost personal power is no** accident. **It is a conscious choice that does not have to be a negative experience.** Without becoming aggressive or cruel, we can reclaim our power in a gentle, firm, and intentional manner to ensure that we maintain the ability to nurture our own needs.

External contributions to our need bowl are still an essential part of achieving balanced fulfillment, but we do not have to give up our personal power to be worthy of support from others. We can choose to offer our bowl to others for contributions while remaining cognizant of our own role in maintaining and supplementing it.

We have the personal power and the responsibility to nurture our own needs.

These are just a few of the ways we can invite love and light into our life while building a strong foundation for noticing and nurturing our needs. Nurturing Self is an imperfect art that improves with practice as we continue to explore the ways to create healthy relationship with Self and others. Each moment of life affords us opportunity to choose healing and growth.

Be a Lifelong Learner

*I was always looking outside myself for strength
and confidence but it comes from within.
It is there all the time.*
ANNA FREUD

Experience and wisdom are the gift of age, but simply accumulating clock and calendar time does not necessarily translate into real personal growth. After years of living, many of us still harbor curiosity about Self and the meaning of life. Whether we are puzzled or just hoping to release untapped potential for more joy and fulfillment in our life, pursuing personal growth through lifelong learning may lead to the answers that already lie within us.

No matter how much we have learned, doors to more wisdom open when we realize how much we still do not know. **Personal growth work is a form of lifelong learning that involves the search for authentic Self through a deeper understanding and a more compassionate view of our inner workings.** Finding the courage and honesty to examine emotional triggers and personal issues helps us learn how to extract hurtful arrows by honoring feelings, nurturing needs, healing old wounds, and accepting Self in a loving way. The resulting peace and centeredness provide many

NURTURE
NEEDS

of us with a new, clearer focus on who we are and what we want in life.

Development of Self is not completely new for people who have pursued lifelong learning within their religious communities, educational institutions, and places of work. Living in relationship with our fellow travelers and struggling with real-time application of all that we have learned continue to serve as our most challenging classroom. For those who are still looking for more, there is a whole new world of information to discover and wisdom to gain by reading books, attending workshops, watching educational films, and listening to teachers and activists.

Therapy and counseling are forms of personal work that provide many of us with guidance and support for growth. Many valuable insights and skills come from wise counseling and point us in the direction of other therapeutic ways to continue our search, either individually or surrounded by supportive, facilitated groups. Like leaves on a great tree, a myriad of new areas of interest, collections of individuals, and self-help groups have sprouted in recent years, as more and more people seek to understand the *why* of their life and relationships. Through a variety of experiential and educational activities, we awaken our consciousness to new possibilities. **Breaking free from unhelpful belief systems and embracing nurturing environments encourage healing and growth.**

Some people may be skeptical or perhaps scared to do work on old issues and do not understand how bringing up wounds from the past could possibly explain pain in the present. Addressing suffering would not be necessary if suppressed emotional energy just went away, but it never does. Unexpressed anger vibrates destructively in our bodies, uncried tears wait to be shed, and shame rides on our back until we choose to use our personal power to learn, heal, and grow.

Our heart is slow to accept new ways, and we often resist the lessons we most need to learn. Doing this work in the presence of others can be a turn-off. However, many people discover that the transformational power of healthy, loving support found in traditional and non-traditional communities can actually reduce the fear of looking deeper within Self.

Past problems can manifest in our present situations, whether we notice them or not. A limited or extreme emotional range, persistent dissatisfaction, or undermining frustrations that make inner harmony ever elusive might be our invitation to slow down and experience the benefits of personal work. **Clearing the past is not about seeking vengeance or blaming and shaming. It is about freeing Self from the insistent grip of the past so that we can fully engage in the present moment.** Whether we are dealing with old wounds or fresh ones,

NURTURE
NEEDS

personal growth work provides a safe way to transform our suffering into healing and growth.

There are many ways to pursue lifelong learning that are valid and contribute to personal growth. Life is more about the journey than the destination. One of the surest paths to understanding Self and creating inner harmony is to open our eyes, mind, and heart along the way.

WAY 5

CREATE INNER HARMONY

*Relationships are intimate arenas in which you encounter
frightened parts of your personality and frightened parts
of the personalities of others. Harmony is the intention
to heal. . . .Harmony is the conscious creation of a loving
world. The intention to create harmony is medicine for
deep pain. It opens you, illuminates your dark places,
brings peace to them, and allows you to develop your
greatest gift – an open heart.*

GARY ZUKAV AND LINDA FRANCIS

My Search

I honor the many ways that people have given their energy and LifeTime to seek enlightenment and peace of mind. My personal search for meaning and harmony has led me to embrace the messiness that comes with actively engaging in everyday human relationships. Although my original quest for harmony was based on achieving a fantasy of idealized characters and circumstances, the authentic inner harmony that I eventually found has proven to be much different from this dream.

My youth and early adulthood were filled with confusion, contradiction, and conflict that pulled me in opposing directions about who I was and who I should be. On one hand, I was being taught kindness and forgiveness. On the other, I was exhorted to fight and compete with other young boys on the sports field. During my teenage years, I lost an older cousin to suicide, and my resulting feelings of grief were never fully experienced or even discussed with my family. I harbored feelings of fear and anger as I witnessed a world buffeted by the contradictions and conflicts of the civil rights movement and the winds of the Viet Nam War. My search for personal identity and purpose, like many young people of the day was further complicated by the expectation to do great things and make lots of money. All these factors came together in a powerful turmoil that kept me off balance and disrupted any sense of inner harmony I had been able to realize.

In those days, I had a tendency to rely on other people to define me and determine my level of harmony, or lack thereof. I was under great pressure by family, society, and school to be someone I was not, and I received little guidance on how to be true to my Self. Reflecting on the chaos of those times, I could have been a poster child for disharmony. I now realize that my understanding of harmony was limited to its use as a musical term, not as a desired state of being for a mature, adult human being.

Years later, I received two insightful lessons about harmony. My first was that external harmony begins with internal harmony. The second lesson was even more significant, because I realized that I had the power to encourage that internal harmony through my own choices. This knowledge did not come easily. Only after having endured and inflicted much pain in my closest relationships did I start down a path of reconciliation and healing that would lead me to more inner harmony.

My first marriage revealed my emotional and spiritual immaturity, a direct result of my dysfunctional family background and my active addictive behaviors. Blaming and shaming my wife for our relationship problems eventually led us to divorce, proving how clueless I was about healthy relationship. The next ten years I spent trying to grow up and to learn more about how to resolve my inner conflicts, fears, and anger.

Through the grace of a power greater than Self, I began to make personal choices that fostered positive change and growth. This was a subtle but total transformation from my supposed-to-be Self into my more real and authentic Self. Slowly but surely this new me experienced greater degrees of inner harmony. I became a more sober, centered person, who could confidently and consciously seek a more compatible partner. I was hopeful that my next marriage would be different.

As I began to live my life with more connection and spirituality, I realized that love had the power to heal. I felt ready for a new beginning and a new relationship. Eventually, I met and married a wonderful woman whom I love very much. We happily share the responsibility of parenting our wonderful, beautiful daughter, even as we continue our personal growth work to find internal and external harmony. To this day, my wife and I still struggle with the challenges of supporting each other as we learn, heal, and grow. My old habit of blaming my partner for any relationship problems is sometimes hard to resist. Fortunately, the mirror of our marriage provides the opportunity to see even deeper into my own woundedness.

After many years of searching, I am learning that my inner harmony is a relative state of being, not an absolute one. I can achieve some harmony, but my old fantasy of idealized circumstances is not real or sustainable. There are things over which I have no power, and my serenity depends on my ability to accept that reality. Now I understand that there are some nurturing changes I can choose to make, like my choice to be more fully present, forgiving, and loving. My ability to surrender to love, grieve for loss, live more simply, and connect with my spiritual nature helps me reconcile inner conflicts, soothe my dis-ease, and create more inner harmony.

There is evidence in my life today that I am a more loving, nurturing man doing my work. My family and I deal with our problems in more constructive, nurturing ways. My relationship with my brother has been reclaimed by mutual love, respect, and support. My goal in life is not to achieve some ideal; rather, it is to be content with what I have. My marriage, parenting my daughter, connecting with 12-Step groups, sharing with my Mankind group, and participating in activist work, especially HEAL, help me stay centered and connected. In this place, at this moment, I know how to get the love I need to experience more inner harmony than I ever thought possible.

Way 5: Create Inner Harmony

*Happiness is when what you think, what you say,
and what you do are in harmony.*
MAHATMA GANDHI

On our inward journey, we have explored one aspect of Self after another. Now we can look at how these elements of relationship with Self come together in ways that help us achieve inner harmony. Discovering how to honor our feelings and how to nurture our needs connects the interrelated and interdependent parts of Self into a more whole, healed, and restored person. We are then able to experience inner harmony, the healthy state of being that occurs when the essential, internal components of who we actually are come into alignment to form a more complete and pleasing arrangement of the Self we aspire to be.

External harmony in relationships and life is often a reflection of a more serene, internal state. **We have little personal power to eliminate the ups and downs of life, but we have many choices that promote the inner stability and centeredness that can empower us to ride out life's inevitable challenges.** Loving and nurturing choices can maintain our balance as we navigate the ebb and flow of our feelings and needs.

Harmony is the feeling we experience when our need bowl is full of loving energy. Unfortunately, this state is temporary and more easily disrupted than created or maintained. We can make choices that corrupt our inner harmony in numerous ways. Misguided intentions and unconscious actions, like attempts to exert power or control over people and events, are as disruptive to our harmony as they are fruitless. Sometimes our harmony is lost when we become more passive or fear-centered. For example, holding on to old resentments or dwelling in unresolved grief can quietly undermine our sense of well-being and peace.

Inner harmony describes an optimal state of being that spontaneously occurs when we spend less time and energy pursuing disruptive choices. The moment we start making more loving and nurturing choices by raising our consciousness, finishing forgiveness, surrendering, accepting, simplifying, and returning to love, we create more inner harmony. These choices allow us to accept reality and address many of our perceived issues or problems.

Aligning all aspects of Self into an integral whole being creates a powerful, stable center from which painful times can be endured and peaceful ones can be celebrated and used for replenishment. As our search finally leads us to our real Self, we see our loving nature as if for the first time. From this place of inner wholeness and harmony, we come to know our own magnificence and are ready to seek the magnificence in others.

Raise Conciousness

When you change the way you look at things,
the things you look at change.
WAYNE DYER

Consciousness of Self is internal awareness of our collective identity. Being conscious literally means being more awake and aware of who we are and what is happening within us and around us at any given moment. Raising our consciousness promotes inner harmony by expanding our awareness of the previously unnoticed and unappreciated details of our inner and outer workings.

The deeper meaning of our behaviors, thoughts, feelings, and needs are revealed to the more conscious Self. Informed with this knowledge and understanding, we are more likely to perceive the things that disrupt our inner harmony, and we become more aware of the choices we can make to restore it. The degree to which we are awake and aware profoundly affects the quality of our perceptions and experiences. Being more fully focused on what is happening in the present moment increases our sensitivity to the significance and richness of the gifts we bring to the world and the wounds we have received.

Like musicians who synchronize individual notes and rhythm into a musical harmony, we can consciously bring together all of our unique pieces and rhythm into a harmony of Self. **Inner harmony is the pleasing, congruent arrangement of all our parts into a whole Self that is greater than the sum of the individual physical, mental, emotional, and spiritual components.**

As a more conscious Self, we are aware of the hurt, resentments, and unfinished forgiveness that is at the source of our anger, the unmet needs that drive our ambition to prove ourselves, or the sadness of the unwelcome grief that undermines the joy of the moment. Life is made up of challenging events for which we are ill prepared. Hence, many of us are compelled or seduced into hiding, denying, or suppressing all or part of these experiences. Harmony is fostered by our ability to allow all our experiences to run their course. Attempting to restrict, control, or limit our awareness or the experience makes us less than whole and feeds disharmony.

Sometimes simplifying our lifestyles and doing less rather than more make us more conscious. Slowing down, getting centered, and focusing calmly on the less obvious aspects of just being can help us recognize and reflect on the meaning and value of each part of Self. When we become keen observers of our feelings, needs, and spiritual nature, the full range of our humanness comes out of the shadows and into the brighter mosaic of real Self.

We experience a more conscious, loving relationship with Self when we stop hiding and start embracing all of who we are. Even though life may be full of turbulence and turmoil, the more parts of Self we consciously bring into the light, the more we nurture the peaceful accord of inner harmony.

CREATE
INNER
HARMONY

Surrender

Life has its own rhythm. If you are surrendered,
you will find it. But surrendering is not easy.
PAUL FERRINI

Turning over our illusion of choice to a power
greater than Self is a simple act of trust known
as surrender. Acceptance of our powerlessness is not only
the beginning of finding our real power; it is one of the
choices we can make to create inner harmony.

In cultures that equivocate anything less than victory
to failure, trusting a positive outcome to surrender is too
risky and difficult to be considered practical. **Letting go
of fear, surrendering our will to win or to always have
the right answers, and relinquishing control over certain
situations are choices that are counterintuitive to many
people's training and preparation for life.**

What is the risk of making the choice to surrender?
Are we afraid to surrender because we might lose control,
artificial security, or superficial love or because we might
achieve real power, reasonable safety, and authentic,
loving relationships? Getting what we really need for Self
is sometimes more frightening than giving up the endless
struggle to maintain what we fear we might lose. Surrender
is a choice that can free us from the seduction of this
struggle and the weight of its burden. This freedom allows

us to experience an immediate sense of relief and calm the moment we surrender.

Disharmony often occurs because we resist the natural flow of life. Instead of imposing our own sense of timing on people or events, the drumbeat of life can guide us, if we will only listen to it. If we are not in tune with the tempo of life, its cues are easy to miss. Synchronizing with life's rhythm is easier when awareness of our own rhythm is raised. Like the dancer who surrenders to the beat of the music, our life unfolds more gracefully when we surrender to the flow rather than move against it.

Sometimes we impose actual negative consequences and disrupt our own harmony by making choices that are intended to minimize distress. Many of us will experience deep emotional loss, physical discomfort, or abusive relationship interactions at some time in our lives. The loss of a child or spouse, surviving an accident or a serious illness, losing our ability to see, hear, or work are some examples of negative experiences that may cause such profound and permanent change that we are never able to view Self or life in exactly the same way again. **The practice of surrender invites us to accept, even embrace, suffering as an inevitable part of life.**

Once we understand that no defense mechanisms are strong enough and no belief walls sturdy enough to keep out hardship, we realize how impractical it is to believe we have the power to prevent pain and suffering. Surrendering to the fact that we will experience joy and pain during our lifetime helps us embrace both when they arrive. By allowing the experience and pursuing healing, our inner harmony and wholeness eventually will return.

To some people, surrender may seem like cowardly inaction. However, surrender is actually a choice for action that requires courage, determination, and energy. Another common misperception of surrender characterizes letting go as impractical, lazy, and dishonorable. These attitudes are inaccurate and discourage us from giving surrender an opportunity to work in our lives.

Sometimes we resist surrender because of our strong attachments and expectations to desired outcomes. Miraculously, many have found that a need may get met when we let go, even though it is not always met in the way anticipated or hoped for initially.

If we resist the chance to resolve a problem, we maintain the struggle and our suffering. Resistance lures us with unrealistic promises, while coaxing us to achieve the impossible. Rather than continue our futile efforts to live up to unrealistic expectations, we can choose to surrender. Inner harmony happens when we stop resisting, start dancing to life's rhythm, and experience the relief, calm, and peace of surrender.

Finish Forgiveness

If we really want to love, we must learn how to forgive.
MOTHER THERESA

The choice to defend or retaliate may be a protective reflex to an attack or injury, but people have been slow to realize that these options do not effectively serve to maintain or restore harmony. A loving alternative to vengeance or resentment is forgiveness.

Forgiveness of our transgressors is easier said than done. This process usually involves a healing journey that begins with forgiveness of Self and ends with the courageous choice to let go of blaming others and to release our own guilt. Learning forgiveness of Self is a relatively fresh and untried path we can choose that allows us to regain our own integrity and renew our inner harmony.

Like fear, guilt is a feeling that has its usefulness. Guilt is a shameful feeling that makes us aware of harmful, often unintended, consequences of certain choices before we make them. At other times, shameful feelings sweep over us after a choice has been made. Long after guilt has served its useful purpose, many of us hold on to our shame and use it as an oppressive form of self-punishment intended to insure we pay for any thoughts or behaviors that could cause suffering, harm, or negative consequences. Destructive, self-imposed condemnation imprisons us and wastes valuable life energy. Hauling around a burden of regret, resentment, or revenge impairs our personal growth and harmony.

Whether intentional or accidental, transgressions and offenses cause a loss of love, integrity, and harmony. **Forgiveness of Self means seeing our accountability for our choices, accepting our responsibility for making them, dealing with the consequences, and learning from the experience.** When we choose to let go of blame and guilt associated with the past, restoration of fullness begins, and we can then live in more conscious, capable ways.

Harmful behaviors are often the result of hurts and wounds that we come by honestly through no fault of our own. Dealing constructively with these wounds gives us insight into Self and reminds us of our innocent origins. **Forgiving Self for not being the person others would have us be, for not being perfect, or for not being that supposed-to-be person are nurturing choices that replace inner feelings of loathing with love and harmony.**

Forgiveness is not always complete or genuine. In order to make peace and smooth out problems, people frequently verbalize forgiveness but do not truly let go of blaming others or shaming Self. As we attempt to heal and resume normal relations, this unfinished forgiveness separates us from others and reinforces our own perception of inadequacy.

Finishing forgiveness is essential to our long-term health and harmony. This loving action devotes a healing portion of life energy to mitigating the harm done to us by others or that we may have caused by our choices and behaviors. Closure welcomes the life lessons learned that are meant especially for us. This instilled wisdom guides us to make more loving and nurturing choices at the next opportunity. Finishing forgiveness is a loving choice of unconditional acceptance that puts the past behind us, returns us to wholeness, and clears the way for inner harmony.

CREATE
INNER
HARMONY

Welcome Grief

Grief is the normal and natural reaction to loss of any kind,
but we have all been ill prepared to deal with it. Grief is
about a broken heart, not a broken brain.
JOHN W. JAMES AND RUSSELL FRIEDMAN

Loss is another way our inner harmony is disrupted. Grief is the process of fully experiencing our loss and regaining our inner harmony. Grief is a natural part of life that results from a broken heart caused by the loss of a source of love. When we lose something precious to us, whether it is a person, job, place, or pet, we lose a part of Self, leaving us feeling less than whole. How can we have inner harmony when we are no longer whole? The answer is simple; we cannot. **Grief is a process that heals our heart and Self back to wholeness through slow, patient, loving restoration.**

We rarely welcome grief and sadness. **To some people, grieving may seem like useless suffering rather than meaningful healing, because the healing purpose of grief is unclear and the accompanying suffering and pain are not easy to endure.** Denial and resistance are more common reactions to loss, because we find it hard to accept that someone or something that was such a part of our life is really gone. Welcoming grief and embracing all aspects of the suffering that happen around loss are the surest ways to complete a return to wholeness and move beyond loss.

Loss deprives our need bowls of the precious love needed from a particular source. The void left by a lost father, mother, sibling, partner, or child may cause many feelings to well up from time to time for the rest of our lives, even after we appear to have healed and moved beyond the initial grief. If our relationships have included less than loving words or deeds, these unresolved interactions form the core of our grief and the resulting feelings never go away, even if ignored or covered up. Our recovery from loss depends on finding creative, loving ways to resolve past relationship issues. Honoring our feelings of grief clears negative, emotional energy, and restores our harmony.

Loss can generate large amounts of intense emotional energy for extended periods of time. During grief, we may experience a roller coaster ride of feelings with many ups, downs, and sharp turns. Glad feelings may arise from our memories of good times, only to be pushed aside as we are racked with anger, sadness, fear, or shame about experiences that left us feeling less than.

Grieving can be a long, difficult process that requires many emotions to be embraced. One loss begets another. The first casualties are our glad feelings of happiness, joy, and contentment. At a later point, a significant decline in appetite, energy level, motivation, and aliveness occurs, having a devastating effect on our health, functionality, and inner harmony. No matter how unpleasant, welcoming our grief means fully embracing, in healthy and constructive ways, whatever comes up around our losses in the present moment. Grief challenges us to clarify and ask for what we needed in the past but were not able to obtain.

Reliving past relationships by fully experiencing grief in our own way heals us back to wholeness and harmony. When we welcome grief and all that the process encompasses, we find the love we need to survive, achieve completion, and ultimately move beyond loss.

CREATE
INNER
HARMONY

Choose to Live Simply

Live simply so others can simply live.
(ATTRIBUTED TO) MAHATMA GANDHI

The power of simplicity allows us to experience peacefulness. Making choices to live more simply helps us become more conscious, serene, and quiet, counterbalancing the chaos and stress of a fast-paced life. Simplifying releases us from the busyness of daily entanglements.

Families and friends, even pets, place many demands on our time, compounding the complexity of living in a hectic world. In our deadline-oriented culture, material things and *to do lists* extract a share of our precious LifeTime. Taking care of houses, yards, gardens, cars, boats, bikes, and businesses adds stress to our day and affects us mentally, emotionally, physically, and spiritually. **Our life becomes the sum total of what holds our attention and receives our energy.**

One cost of doing too much is having less harmony. Too many relationships, responsibilities, and commitments can make our life more complex and distracting. Many people make these complicating choices because, despite the price of a busy life, these activities can still be rewarding and beneficial. Balancing the cost of a demanding work schedule, a longer commute, a higher mortgage, or a fancier

CREATE
INNER
HARMONY

car with the benefits of more money, prestige, comfort, or convenience can be exhausting and confusing in a culture full of mixed signals about what is desirable and what is not. **Placing value on our peace of mind, more time with loved ones, or just experiencing less stress are questionable choices in a world that relies so heavily on materialistic measuring sticks.**

Less can be more. Getting what we really need right now might be easier than we think, especially if our need for more is driven by a belief that more is better. How much is enough? The reality is we can probably still enjoy life by having a little less money, fewer things, and sometimes fewer people in our life, although these can be challenging choices to make. Incentives for living more simply are measured in qualitative rewards, not numbers.

Simplifying our life clears inner space for spending time with a loved one, a sick friend, our higher power, or our developing Self. Slowing down and living consciously in the present moment create inner harmony that moves with us wherever we go. The fear of not being good enough or lovable can push us to control other people or events over which we have no power, creating stress and anxiety in the process. Letting go of the need to do all the things we believe are necessary to be loved frees us of this fear. Giving up the assumption we have to fix everyone and everything brings simplicity and peace.

Surrendering to a power greater than Self to provide all we need and trusting in the competence of others to take care of themselves free us to simply live. A more meaningful, less-complicated life fosters inner harmony.

CREATE
INNER
HARMONY

Be Gentle with Our Self

*Children who are not loved in their very beingness do not
know how to love themselves. As adults, they have to learn
to nourish, to mother their own lost child.*
MARION WOODMAN

The challenges of life can be difficult enough
without our being hard on Self. Rather than
accept that bad things just happen in our lives, too often
we are our worst critics. **We react to events by telling
ourselves we are somehow bad, unworthy, less than, or
just not good enough. Based on twisted interpretations of
the facts, these harsh, unkind self-messages cast a shadow
of inadequacy, robbing us of our inner harmony.**

Fortunately, when we do our inner work and bring light
to these previously hidden assumptions and beliefs, they can
be dissipated, dispelled, and undone. On the path to find
real Self, it is possible to see and understand these internal
communications and how they can be used to promote
change for the good. **Gentle, kind, and reassuring
messages of Self-talk replace the old taskmaster with a
compassionate voice that gently blesses and forgives.**

Being gentle with our Self affirms our worth and
prevents additional harm. Our own gentle hand, one
that comforts and supports us on the journey, shapes our
inner harmony.

Return to Love

And the end of all our exploring
Will be to arrive where we started
And know the place for the first time.
T.S. ELIOT

In the beginning, we are a part of something greater than Self. At the moment of separation from this harmonious whole, we begin to experience disharmony caused by the roughness of the world. Like a pinch of the sun, our essence is a bit of pure light and love encapsulated in a tiny, delicate human package. Despite a miraculous design as the perfect host for its spiritual guest, the human body serves as a coarse vessel for the exquisitely sensitive essence of Self, a vessel vulnerable to pain and discomfort.

Emerging into a world of relationships, we struggle to adapt and survive in an environment that can be less than loving and nurturing. **Even when surrounded by the healthiest, most loving and supportive individuals, groups, and families, we experience a wide variety of spiritual bumps, bruises, and wounds. The sting of these injuries slowly replaces the fading memories of our perfect origin and impinges on the core of our loving and spiritual Self.**

We grow into adolescence and adulthood with some

emotional and spiritual damage that is usually reinforced by powerful, fear-centered, subliminal reminders of past anger, shame, and disappointment. These silent messages sculpt the supposed-to-be Self, diminishing the light and eclipsing the beauty of real Self.

Our loss of childhood innocence and capacity for unconditional love are usurped by choices intended to protect us from the perceived demands of relationship and intimacy. Instead, these defensive skills can isolate and paralyze us, and we find real Self further separated from the love we desire.

Like a genie imprisoned in a bottle, our internal being remains pure and innocent, although it is more confined than comfortable. We lose touch with the true nature of Self as a loving being. **Separation from our essence of love is the greatest cause for loss of inner harmony.**

The stress and tension in our life reflect disharmony that motivates us to ask the essential, universal questions about identity, origin, and purpose. We sense that something known long ago has now been lost or forgotten, so we resume an exhausting, external search for Self and meaning. Inevitably, the circle of life brings us back to an unexplored place, the internal world of Self. Here we remember many amazing things and learn others that we did not know we did not know.

In the end we arrive back where we began, before we lost the awareness of what has always existed. We realize that Self is more than mere thoughts in our heads alone. Self is a whole being experience that includes feelings and needs. When we invite and accept all parts of Self, inner harmony gently washes over us. Self not only needs to give and receive love, **Self is love.**

Love is our nature and our greatest need is to be aligned with love. Each of us is a small piece of loving energy that yearns to be connected to a loving whole that is greater than Self. Could this longing explain our yearning to connect to a higher power and to be in meaningful relationships with all living creatures? By accessing the love within Self, we establish a cornerstone for creating loving connection with others. Our purpose is not to completely understand all of love's mysteries but simply to live as beings of love.

At the end of all our exploring, we return to our beginning and know Self as if for the first time, as we have been all along – a loving, spiritual being walking a human path.

233

There is so much left to know,
And I am on the road to find out.
YUSAF ISLAM

With Gratitude

A book is never the product of its author alone. In so many ways, I am merely serving as a conduit to connect the wisdom and knowledge of others with the curiosity and needs of my fellow travelers. I am grateful for the many loving, trusted friends who were so generous with their time and expertise to dialogue and listen to me as this book was created. Here is my humble, heartfelt attempt to acknowledge all those whose willingness to share their experience, strength, and hope made my learning, healing, and growth possible and whose generosity supported the creation of this book.

To my Higher Power, who graces me with the serenity to accept the things I cannot change and empowers me to change the things I can.

To those valued collaborators who read, challenged, and nurtured the book: Otis and Fredericka Carney, Randy Gamble, Gwynne Carter, Ron Savarese, Brad Zahn, Lisa Miller, Rhonda Hidaji, Steve Charles, Kaveh Safa, John McDonnell, Ellen Kleiner, Morris Klass, Jean Handley, Ann Smithwick, Nicky and Ellen Strange, Jim and Kay Dickerson, Steve Pike, Hank DeFelice, and Angela Less.

To great teachers and role models who bless this work, like Don Jones, Louise Diamond, John Lee, John James, Karen Riss, and Patricia Sun.

To Victor La Cerva, for his thoughtful Foreword, for his friendship, and for mentoring and inspiring me by his example.

To my editor, writing partner, and co-worker at HEAL, Janette Hester, an artist in her own right, for knowing when to push and when to relax, so that my inner guidance could transform my experiences into words.

To my good friend Gary Rosenberg, for sharing with me in so many ways his wisdom and love while on the journey.

To my co-worker and aikido student, Sharaze Colley, for her tireless efforts to shape and refine the content layout into the book you now hold in your hand. She is like a daughter to me and amazes me daily with her energy, willingness, and courage to explore life.

To the artists, Kerry Peeples and Pam Santirojprapai, whose exceptional talents and gifts combined to create the beautiful images on the cover and the pages of this book.

Many thanks to Janette Serdar, Raney Azada, and Paula Gaither for their enthusiasm and hard work that make the work of HEAL possible.

To the men in the Mankind Project, especially those in

my I-Group, who serve as an essential community for me. Here I am able to find and heal my Self, while realizing my mission to love and nurture others.

To the many, many people in my 12-Step groups who have nurtured me over the years by sharing their struggles and stories while patiently listening to mine and loving me anyway.

To Morehei Ueshiba, O Sensei, for creating Aikido; to my Aikido community in Memphis; to my sensei Hugh Young, who showed me how to be strong and gentle at the same time; to Rick Beredini, my sempai and sponsor, to the wonderful folks at Utah Aikikai; and to Frank Doran and Cynthia Hayashi, the head and heart of California Aikido Association.

To all the members of Aiki Extensions, especially Donald Levine, George Leonard, and Wendy Palmer, for showing me how to take Aikido off the mat and into the world.

To Calvary Church and the wonderful people who have been my family's faith community for five generations. Especially to Doug Bailey, Andy McBeth, the men in my prayer group, and the folks in the breakfast club.

And, most importantly, to my own family: my late father Stephan, my mother Demetria, and my brothers, John and Ted. Your love and courage inspire my life.

Special love and blessings to my wife Corinne and daughter Madeleine, who supply me with constant love, acceptance, patience, and comic relief while I wrestle with this work.

And finally . . . much appreciation to you, the reader, for your interest, courage, and desire to seek your authentic Self. May this book remind you of the humility and magnificence of being a human Self.

Bibliography

Alcoholics Anonymous. Pocket Edition, 2004.

Bender, Sue. *Every Day is Sacred: A Woman's Journey Home*. Harper San Francisco, 1995.

Bradshaw, John. *Homecoming: Reclaiming and Championing Your Inner Child*. Bantam Books, 1990.

Branden, Nathaniel. *Six Pillars of Self-Esteem*. Bantam Books, 1994.

Brussat, Frederic and Mary Ann. *Spiritual Literacy: Reading the Sacred in Everyday Life*. Simon and Schuster Inc., 1996.

Casey, Karen and Martha Vanceburg. *The Promise of a New Day: A Book of Daily Meditations*. HarperCollins, 1983.

Chopra, Deepak. *The Path to Love*. Harmony Books, 1997.

Chopra, Deepak. *The Seven Spiritual Laws of Success*. San Rafael Calif.: New World Library, 1994.

Cousins, Norman. *Anatomy of an Illness*. New York: Norton, 1979.

Diamond, Louise. *The Peace Book*. Conari Press, 2001.

De Mello, Anthony. *Awareness: The Perils and Opportunities of Reality*. Doubleday, 1992.

Dyer, Wayne. *There's a Spiritual Solution to Every Problem*. HarperCollins Publishers, 2001.

Eldredge, John. *Wild at Heart: Discovering the Secret to a Man's Soul*. Nelson Books, 2001.

Exley, Helen. *Wisdom of the Millennium*. Exley Publications Ltd. In Great Britain, 1999.

Ferrini, Paul. *The Bridge to Reality*. 1990.

Godek, Gregory. *Love: The Course They Forgot to Teach You in School*.
Casablanca Press, 1997.

Hay, Louise L. *The Power is Within You*. Hay House, Inc., 1991.

Hendricks, Gay and Kathlyn Hendricks. *Conscious Loving: The Journey to Co-Commitment*. Bantam Books, 1992.

James, John W. and Russell Friedman. *The Grief Recovery Handbook*. Harper Row Publishers, 1998 revised.

Jampolsky, Gerald. *Love is Letting Go of Fear*. Celestial Arts, 1979.

Jones, Don. *Wisdom for the Journey*. Two Snakes Publishing, 2000.

Kane, Ray and Nancy. *From Fear to Love: Overcoming the Barriers to Healthy Relationships*. Moody, 2002.

La Cerva, Victor. *Pathways to Peace: Forty Steps to a Less Violent America*. HEAL Foundation Press, 1996.

La Cerva, Victor. *Worldwords: Global Reflections to Awaken the Spirit*. HEAL Foundation Press, 1999.

Lee, John. *Facing the Fire: Experiencing and Expressing Anger Appropriately*. Bantam Books, 1993.

London, Jack. *To Build a Fire*. Bantam Books, 1988.

M.A.F. Touchstones: A Book of Daily Meditations for Men. HarperCollins, 1986

Miller, Fred. *How to Calm Down, Even If You Are Completely and Totally Nuts: A Simple Guide to Relaxation*. Namaste Press, 1999.

Millman, Dan. *Way of the Peaceful Warrior: A Book that Changes Lives*. HJ Kramer, Inc., 1980.

Moore, Thomas. *Care of the Soul: A Guide for Cultivating Depth and Sacredness in Everyday Life*. HarperCollins Publishers, 1992.

Palmer, Wendy. *The Intuitive Body*. North Atlantic Books, 1991.

Papalia, Diane E., Sally Wendkos Olds, and Ruth Duskin Feldman. *Human Development*. McGraw-Hill, 1998.

Rilke, Rainer Marie. *Letters To A Young Poet, Letter Six, December 1903*. Translation by Stephen Mitchell.

Kubler-Ross, Elisabeth. *On Death and Dying*. Touchstone, 1969.

Rogers, Fred. *You Are Special: Neighborly Wisdom from Mister Rogers*. Running Press Book Publishers, 2002.

Rogers, Philip. *Do You Feel Loved By Me?* Living Well Publications, 1999.

Rosenberg, Gary. *Too Tight To Touch Your Toes*. Yoga DVD, 2005.

Rosenberg, Marshall B. *Nonviolent Communication: A Language of Compassion*. PuddleDancer Press, 2002.

Tolle, Eckhart. *The Power of Now: A Guide to Spiritual Enlightenment*. Namaste Publishing Inc., 1997.

Woodman, Marion. *Addiction to Perfection*. Toronto: Inner City Books, 1982.

Zukav, Gary and Linda Francis. *The Mind of the Soul: Responsible Choice*. Simon and Schuster, Inc., 2003.

Web Resources

healfoundation.org

Grief-Recovery.com

mkp.org

thepeacecompany.com

jlcsonline.com

patriciasun.com

gandhiinstitute.org

turningpointpartners.com

tootightyoga.com

hazelden.org

womanwithin.org

cnvc.org

peacejam.org

newdimensions.org

matthewkelly.org

yourownersmanual.com

totalintegrationinstitute.com

apeacemaker.net

sondraray.com

radicalforgiveness.com

SimpleLiving.org

lifepathretreats.com

al-anon.alateen.org

alcoholics-anonymous.org

floweringmountain.com

cnvc.org

For more links visit www.seekingself.org

About the Artists

Kerry Peeples

For Kerry D. Peeples creating has always been a means of connecting to God and the world around her. "When I create, it's really a pilgrimage, a seeking center, finding that place where I meet God and we make a joyful mess together." A painter, a potter, and a builder, Kerry's art is a reflection of her love of nature and the creative process. Her work includes oil, encaustic, collage, textiles and clay.

Kerry was awarded a BA in painting from Berea College and a Masters in Teaching from the University of Memphis. She lives in Memphis, TN, with her husband and son. (kerrypeeples10@msn.com)

Napapon (Pam) Santirojprapai

A native of Thailand, Pam Santirojprapai has lived in the South for the past twenty years. A homemaker and mother of two sons, she describes her artistic process as one of prayer or praise, a gift from God.

An innate understanding of color and shape emerged following an illness, and Pam began to paint and sculpt. She often uses fabric, metal, and wood as part of her creative medium. Her art content is simple and pure, almost spiritual, and always expressive of Pam's gratitude. Her work is included in the permanent collection of Mississippi Good Will Corporation, and it has been on exhibition in Tennessee, Mississippi, and Louisiana. (cici123art@yahoo.com)

Vicki McLaughlin

A gifted photographer with the uncanny ability to capture the emotions and moods of children and family in her portraits, Vicki has traveled extensively with her camera lens poised to bring spirit to life. For over ten years, her photography business has been located in Memphis, TN, where Vicki resides with her husband Ted and their two children. (vickiMc61@aol.com)

About the Author

Stephan is a devoted son, brother, husband, and father who expresses a deep love for his family and people. An active outdoorsman with a respect for the environment, Stephan lived for many years in Utah, where he enjoyed hiking, biking, snowboarding, and the practice of Aikido, a Japanese martial art. He later founded Aikido at the Center in Memphis, Tennessee, where he continues to practice and teach.

He was a successful entrepreneur and small businessman for 34 years. However, after entering the world of recovery, he was moved to follow his passion for human relationship. For the last 12 years, he has spent more time working in the nonprofit world than the for-profit one. His dedication to seek and share the meaning of healthy relationship inspired him to found the HEAL organization, an educational nonprofit that publishes books and sponsors conferences, workshops, and spiritual events that support positive change.

Today Stephan pursues his life mission to create harmony by loving and nurturing himself and others into wholeness and integrity through his active membership in the Mankind Project and HEAL. This work includes multi-cultural, conflict resolution, and intervention programs and processes. He also collaborates with his associates at HEAL and with other gifted facilitators from around the world to increase awareness of healthy relationship through experiential workshops and community-building groups called Circles.

Married to his beloved wife Corinne for 14 years, they relish the joys of nurturing and the challenges of parenting their young daughter, Madeleine. The family pod also includes a yuppie puppy, Zoe, and two dwarf hamsters, Brownie and Chunky. Stephan currently resides with his family in Memphis, TN.

The mission of HEAL is to promote healthy human relationships through educational and peacemaking information, materials, and programs, in the hope of strengthening the common ground upon which all people can live more joyful, peaceful, and prosperous lives.

HEAL

HEAL GOALS

HEAL is an organization of people who care about people and who are committed to:

Exploring fundamental elements and dynamics of healthy relationships;

Identifying tools and techniques for encouraging loving and nurturing relationships between individuals and their families, friends, and communities;

Promoting healthy relationships by increasing people's awareness and use of these tools and techniques;

Creating positive change by utilizing knowledge and understanding of relationships to assist in conflict resolution, community building, peacemaking, and addressing social issues and problems.

We believe all humans have the desire to increase their own health and happiness and to decrease their suffering. HEAL seeks to affirm and stimulate each individual's capacity to live in healthy relationship. Our work is based on the assumptions that human relationships have similar dynamics and commonalities and that the lack of loving and nurturing relationship skills is at the heart of many pressing and disturbing problems.

We hold the belief that an improved understanding of our basic human characteristics and relationships are essential ingredients in understanding and dealing with many of the problems and challenges faced by individuals, families, societies, and even nations in the world community.

It is not our goal to present some form of ultimate truth. It is our hope that our work will help identify certain aspects of the human family that can be used to increase positive, harmonious relationships while reducing negative, harmful interactions.

Relationship formation and maintenance play major roles in defining us as people. In fact, a vast majority of our time is spent interacting in an incredible number and variety of relationships. Failure to form and sustain healthy relationships can lead to dysfunctional, and sometimes abusive, relationships, which pose fundamental challenges to our individual and communal health.

Relationships are part of all aspects of our lives. We are involved in them at home, on the job, in the car, in our spiritual groups, even when we are alone. Looking at these activities and seeking to understand them better could open a new approach to living life, to connecting and communicating with people, to loving and nurturing those we care about, and to reducing and resolving conflicts with others.

Your interest and support of HEAL and its efforts are greatly appreciated. For more information or to tell us about your important work in this area, please contact us at:

HEAL
Stephan McLaughlin, Jr.
P.O. Box 241209
Memphis, TN 38124-1209
901-320-9179
www.healfoundation.org

Profits from the sale of this book will benefit HEAL, a nonprofit organization dedicated to promoting healthy relationship among people through education, peacemaking, and community building.

Order Form

Order online: www.healfoundation.org
Telephone orders: (901) 320-9179
Postal orders: HEAL, Stephan McLaughlin, P.O. Box 214209, Memphis, TN 38124-1209.

Item	Cost	Quantity
Seeking Self: an inner journey to healthy relationship Stephan McLaughlin, Jr.	$15	_____
Pathways to Peace: Forty Steps to a Less Violent America Victor La Cerva, M.D.	$15	_____
Worldwords: Global Reflections to Awaken the Spirit Victor La Cerva, M.D.	$15	_____
World Without Violence Edited by Dr. Arun Gandhi	$15	_____
Add $3.00 for shipping. Call for quantity discounts.		_____
Total Amount Enclosed		_____

Name: _____

Address: _____

City: _____ State: _____ Zip: _____

Telephone: _____

Email: _____

Payment: ☐ Check   ☐ Credit Card:

☐ Visa   ☐ MasterCard   ☐ American Express

Card Number: _____

Name on Card: _____ Exp. date: _____

Order Form

Order online: www.healfoundation.org
Telephone orders: (901) 320-9179
Postal orders: HEAL, Stephan McLaughlin, P.O. Box 214209, Memphis, TN 38124-1209.

Item	Cost	Quantity
Seeking Self: an inner journey to healthy relationship Stephan McLaughlin, Jr.	$15	_____
Pathways to Peace: Forty Steps to a Less Violent America Victor La Cerva, M.D.	$15	_____
Worldwords: Global Reflections to Awaken the Spirit Victor La Cerva, M.D.	$15	_____
World Without Violence Edited by Dr. Arun Gandhi	$15	_____
Add $3.00 for shipping. Call for quantity discounts.		_____
Total Amount Enclosed		_____

Name: _____

Address: _____

City: _____ State: _____ Zip: _____

Telephone: _____

Email: _____

Payment: ☐ Check ☐ Credit Card:

☐ Visa   ☐ MasterCard   ☐ American Express

Card Number: _____

Name on Card: _____ Exp. date: _____

Order Form

Order online: www.healfoundation.org
Telephone orders: (901) 320-9179
Postal orders: HEAL, Stephan McLaughlin, P.O. Box 214209,
Memphis, TN 38124-1209.

Item	Cost	Quantity
Seeking Self: an inner journey to healthy relationship Stephan McLaughlin, Jr.	$15	_____
Pathways to Peace: Forty Steps to a Less Violent America Victor La Cerva, M.D.	$15	_____
Worldwords: Global Reflections to Awaken the Spirit Victor La Cerva, M.D.	$15	_____
World Without Violence Edited by Dr. Arun Gandhi	$15	_____
Add $3.00 for shipping. Call for quantity discounts.		_____
Total Amount Enclosed		_____

Name: _____

Address: _____

City: _____ State: _____ Zip: _____

Telephone: _____

Email: _____

Payment: ☐ Check   ☐ Credit Card:

☐ Visa   ☐ MasterCard   ☐ American Express

Card Number: _____

Name on Card: _____ Exp. date: _____